100 NIGHTS

OF A LIFETIME

100 NIGHTS
OF A LIFETIME

The World's Ultimate Adventures After Dark

STEPHANIE VERMILLION

NATIONAL GEOGRAPHIC

WASHINGTON, D.C.

CONTENTS

LEFT: Two women in Jaipur hold candles to celebrate Diwali, the festival of lights, observed for five days throughout India (page 92).

PAGES 2-3: The galaxy shows off above Kow Swamp, an archaeological site near Victoria, Australia.

INTRODUCTION

On the last night of a three-week aurora borealis–chasing trip, the weather couldn't have been worse. Thick clouds obscured the Iceland sky. Drizzling rain wouldn't let up. Still, I had a hunch. If I've learned anything during my career reporting on astrotourism—a form of travel centered on admiring celestial sights—it's that you never know how the night will unfold. The nightscapes can change in an instant. That's the magic of after-dark adventures.

After two hours spent cursing raindrops from the parking lot, I spied the first star. Then more stars. The clouds broke, revealing green swirls that exploded into a multi-hour corkscrew of reds, purples, pinks, and blues. This, I told myself, is why I stay up late.

My interest in night adventures began on a star-speckled camping trip in 2010 in Morocco's Sahara desert. That initial starstruck awe morphed into an obsession the first time I watched the northern lights waltz across the sky nearly a decade later. I've since chased those colorful celestial squiggles more times than I can count, from sheep farms in Greenland to the shores of Lake Superior to that kaleidoscopic Iceland aurora in 2023.

My bedtime (or lack thereof) when I'm traveling may raise eyebrows, but to me, the world after dark is always worth the lack of sleep. Growing up in a light-polluted Midwest city, I never knew the stars could shine like they do over the Sahara. Nor did I realize that watching interstellar wonders, such as a meteor shower, would put life, and my tiny place in the incomprehensibly grand universe, into such a grounding perspective.

As astrotourism booms, I'm clearly not the only one seeking solace in the night sky. An estimated 20 million people traveled just to watch the Great American Eclipse in 2017; millions more did the same for the eclipse over North America in 2024. We're seeing a lot more aurora chasers too. And with more than 200 stargazing destinations certified by DarkSky International

BUDGET KEY

We've indicated approximate budgets for every night of a lifetime in these pages. Though prices are subject to change, the following guidelines were used:

$: U.S. $0–50
$$: U.S. $51–200
$$$: U.S. $201–500
$$$$: U.S. $501–2,000
$$$$$: U.S. $2,001+

ABOVE: **The Grand Canyon is spectacular at night, whether seen from its North or South Rim, or from the canyon floor (page 274).**

PAGES 8-9: **Members of the Kaisokah Moko Jumbies perform with fire on the waterfront near San Fernando during Trinidad and Tobago's Carnival (page 384).**

(formerly International Dark-Sky Association), humbling nightscapes like clear views of the Milky Way, which light pollution hides from one-third of humanity, are increasingly within reach. In the pages that follow, we offer a world of opportunity to take in the night sky.

Yet stargazing and aurora hunting merely scratch the surface of the world's nocturnal adventures. From beloved cultural celebrations, such as Thailand's enchanting lantern festivals (page 78), to lesser known marvels, such as the synchronous arrival of hundreds of nesting sea turtles in Panama (page 302), this book highlights 100 diverse after-dark experiences that make it worth staying up late (or rising early).

Adrenaline junkies can go night canyoning through glowworm caves in New Zealand (page 336) and bungee jumping into an inky abyss in Switzerland (page 162). Food lovers will be chomping at the bit to visit culinary hubs

in Ghana (page 24) and Taiwan (page 62), where bustling night markets offer a scrumptious taste of local culture. A treasure trove of wonder awaits wildlife enthusiasts too. Watch and hear the jungle come to life on an Amazonian paddle trip (page 378), spy on the savanna's busiest hours during a twilight safari (page 26), or watch a miraculous coral spawning on a night dive in the Great Barrier Reef (page 324).

These experiences are reason enough to adjust your bedtime, and an opportunity to find new fun in even the most well-trodden escapes. Take the Grand Canyon. Though the world wonder draws nearly five million annual visitors, just one percent spend the night on the canyon floor. (Learn how to be one of the lucky few on page 274.)

Of course, visiting pristine landscapes like our national parks is a privilege. It comes with responsibility. No matter the hour, follow Leave No Trace principles: Stay on marked trails, carry out all that you bring in, and respect wildlife. Use red lights instead of traditional flashlights to aid your night vision and the vision of others around you, including animals. And, for your own after-dark safety, travel in a group or with a local guide whenever possible. Exploring with a community expert can also enrich your trip and, as many of these adventures illustrate, benefit the local community.

Now, it's time to get traveling. I hope these pages spark awe, inspire wonder, and add a couple—or 100—new nighttime adventures to your bucket list.

PART ONE

AFRICA

Quiver trees, a desert-tough variety of the aloe plant, stand like sentinels under the stars in the Namib Desert (page 36).

SAHARA DESERT STARGAZING

Experience a night full of sand and stars.

BUDGET: $$ **WHEN TO GO:** September–April   **ACTIVITY LEVEL:** Intermediate   **GO FOR:** Stargazing

The plunging sun casts a spell on the Sahara desert. Drumbeats echo from the camel-hair tents. Tantalizing tagine aromas waft through the air. A splash of white pinpricks bejeweling the black sky enthrall slack-jawed visitors. A night beneath the starry Sahara sky, most easily enjoyed via Morocco on the desert's western side, is like an oversize serving of soul food. "You feel how small you are, and how grand the universe is," says Adil Belaguid, co-founder and lead guide of My Moroccan Adventure. "It makes you feel great about life itself."

For millennia, nomadic tribes used the stars, moon, and sun to traverse the Sahara's honey-hued dunes, gravel plains, and boundless salt flats. The largest hot desert on Earth at 3.6 million square miles (9.4 million km²), the Sahara spills into 10 African countries, covering close to a third of the continent. Nomads journeyed across the extreme expanse in lines more than 100 camels long, toting salt, ivory, and gold.

Studying the cosmos was essential for navigating this vast, largely landmark-devoid desert. Technologies may have shifted, but stargazing remains a staple desert experience today.

The typical Sahara trip includes a hike or camel ride into the desert followed by a hearty tagine feast and camping in traditional nomadic tents or alfresco sleeps under the stars.

OTHER MARVELS

They may be an ocean apart, but the Sahara desert is integral to the Amazon rainforest's biodiversity. More than 180 million tons (163 million t) of dust drift from the Sahara across the Atlantic to the Amazon, where the debris delivers phosphorous that's essential to the rainforest fauna's survival.

OPPOSITE: With clear skies, chances are high you can see the Milky Way above the Sahara.

PAGES 14–15: A night of stargazing often begins with a camel ride into the Sahara at sunset, followed by a traditional feast.

Desertgoers have two dune systems to choose from. Erg Chebbi, the most popular swath of dunes, is reachable via the town of Merzouga. There are more than 300 camps at the ready, from luxury glamping accommodations to more traditional tents. Tiziri Camp, a colorful Berber-owned accommodation decked in locally made furniture, provides a sustainable escape. It runs entirely on solar power, sources water from its own well, and introduced the area's first water filtration system. After a day of desert exploration, Tiziri hosts lead guests through the highlights of their home skies, from the North Star, which served as a navigational guardrail, to planets and the shimmery Milky Way, which brilliantly shines in this remote, light pollution–free escape.

A more far-flung and traditional option is Erg Chigaga, the country's largest dune channel, reached by a two-hour 4×4 zip across the desert from the village of M'hamid el Ghizlane. With fewer international visitors, this area is largely unchanged by tourism. "In some cases, we run into actual nomads traveling," says Belaguid. "We'll stop our cars, put out a carpet, and make tea."

Upon reaching Erg Chigaga, watch the sunset, then enjoy astronomical sightseeing and the desert sky's fresco of shooting stars. Morocco is close enough to the Equator to spot both the Northern and Southern Hemisphere constellations; low light pollution also makes highlights like the Andromeda galaxy visible. For peak conditions, visit on new-moon nights between September and April.

TANZANIA

KILIMANJARO NIGHT SUMMIT

Reach Africa's tallest peak on a strenuous starlit climb.

BUDGET: $$$$$ **WHEN TO GO:** January–March or June–October   **ACTIVITY LEVEL:** Strenuous   **GO FOR:** Adventure

S tep, step, breathe. Step, step, breathe. It's a staccato rhythm you'll become all too familiar with after six straight hours hiking beneath the stars to Kilimanjaro's 19,340-foot (5,895 m) Uhuru Peak. The full trek up Africa's tallest mountain requires at least a week, and the mid-trip's midnight-to-sunrise summit schlep is undoubtedly the most challenging—and memorable—night.

Kilimanjaro expeditions begin with moderate jaunts through the stratovolcano's lower-elevation vegetation zones, from montane forest to moorland. The air thins as you ascend; the trying final miles to Uhuru base camp, around 15,000 feet (4,570 m), are a sample of the rigorous overnight peak attempt on the horizon. The goal: Reach the top by sunrise.

On summit night, you'll huff and puff up Mount Kilimanjaro's ashy switchbacks. On clear nights, twinkling stars and a zigzag of headlamps light the way. Gaze skyward for a mental distraction. Up on these high-altitude slopes, the stars look brighter and closer—almost at eye level, like you're trekking into space. Stargazing sights, such as vivid Sirius, the iridescent Milky Way, or the Orion constellation, sparkle just as vividly as they did when the mountain welcomed its first official climbers in the late 1800s.

When nightscapes alone won't mask the pain, intermittent milestones like Gilman's Point at 18,638 feet (5,681 m), then Stella Point at 18,885 feet

CRITTER CORNER

Kilimanjaro climbers often see blue and colobus monkeys, and the nocturnal bush baby on the lower-altitude stints of their climbs. Small numbers of elephants and African buffalo also roam the montane forest at the base, although sightings are rare for trekkers.

OPPOSITE: The last stretch of a trek up Kilimanjaro begins late at night so you reach the summit in time to watch the sunrise.

PAGES 18-19: Camp among—or above—the clouds in your outpost on Kilimanjaro.

(5,756 m), provide a chance to rest, refuel, and skygaze some more before hitting the steep trail again.

As first light spills over the horizon, the stratovolcano's snowy surroundings come into view—as does the Uhuru Peak marker. Your full night of climbing ends with about 30 minutes of awe and celebration atop the Roof of Africa. It may be tempting, but hanging up here much longer could amplify altitude sickness. Plus, a well-earned feast and sleeping bag beckon you back to base camp.

Kilimanjaro is the most attainable of the world's Seven Summits (the tallest peak on each continent). It requires no technical climbing, just endurance, mental toughness, and adequate acclimatization time. That said, it's no easy feat.

Around 30,000 climbers attempt this world-famous volcano annually. Only two-thirds of climbers reach Uhuru Peak; the others fall victim to altitude sickness or must turn around due to weather.

To avoid the former, choose a longer trip with at least seven total days on the mountain. The Lemosho Route, just over 40 total miles (64 km) long, winds through all five of Kilimanjaro's ecosystems, from hot savanna and rainforest to the icy volcanic summit. This jaunt requires camping, and boasts one of the highest success rates, with a steady climb-high, sleep-low acclimatization approach. Hut-to-hut Marangu is a popular choice for those who'd rather sleep in a shelter. It spans 45 total miles (72 km) and offers one of the gentlest grades to the peak.

VICTORIA FALLS MOONBOW

Catch a lunar rainbow over one of Earth's largest waterfalls.

BUDGET: $$ **WHEN TO GO:** February–August   **ACTIVITY LEVEL:** Mild   **GO FOR:** Nature

It's hard to comprehend Victoria Falls' enormity. The thunderous curtain of water stretches more than a mile (1.6 km) between Zimbabwe and Zambia. During the region's high-water season, February to August, the cascade pours 300,000 gallons (1.1 million L) of the Zambezi River down its basalt edge every second. It's a wonder of the natural world and a top southern Africa tourist attraction. Yet, few visitors have seen its after-dark sensation, the lunar rainbow.

On sunny day visits to Victoria Falls, you're highly likely to see a rainbow. The lunar version of the marvel, however, is much less common and requires perfect conditions. Like a rainbow, a moonbow forms when light refracts through water droplets in the air. But rather than sunlight, the catalyst of daytime rainbows, nighttime arcs require radiation from a bright full moon, unobscured by light pollution or clouds.

A moonbow also requires a strong, steady mist. Victoria Falls has its fair share of that. On its most powerful days, the waterfall's plunge creates a sky-high spray that's visible up to 30 miles (48 km) away.

Even if all the conditions align, the lunar rainbow will appear much fainter than its daytime counterpart. That's because the sun is 400,000 times brighter than a full moon. A rainbow has colors we can see with the naked eye, but the dimmer moon's arc looks more like a streak of white.

OPPOSITE: A Victoria Falls moonbow reflects lighter colors than a daytime rainbow and is harder to see with the naked eye.

PAGES 22-23: By day, stand on the rim of Victoria Falls in what's known as the Devil's Pool.

To enhance the view, photograph it with a mirrorless, DSLR, or even smartphone camera; all three are more sensitive to light (and color) than our eyes.

Victoria Falls is only one of a handful of waterfalls in the world that produces this after-dark spectacle. You can spot it on either side of the waterfall, although Zambia has an edge. The Eastern Cataract, one of Zambia's most popular daytime waterfall overlooks, is ideal because the moon will be at your back. On the Zimbabwean side, head to overlook seven, the Devil's Cataract, for the best vantage point.

On the night of a full moon (and just before and after), both sides of the park remain open until midnight for lunar rainbow chasers; an entry fee is still required. Sightings are most likely from February to August, when the water levels have peaked.

WHILE YOU'RE THERE

Get your heart pumping: Bungee jump from the Victoria Falls Bridge, which connects Zambia and Zimbabwe, for a 360-foot (110 m) free fall toward the crocodile-filled Zambezi River. Tours run via Shearwater Bungee and are reachable from both countries.

OSU NIGHT MARKET

Sample street food at Ghana's historic twilight hangout.

BUDGET: $–$$ **WHEN TO GO:** Year-round **ACTIVITY LEVEL:** Mild **GO FOR:** Local bites

Heading to Ghana? Be sure to pack your appetite. Culinary marvels abound in this West African nation, but few places dish them out like Accra's Osu Night Market.

The bustling market, located in the capital city's Osu neighborhood, has tempted Ghanaians and visitors with traditional, zesty bites for centuries. Historians date it to the 17th-century construction of the nearby Christiansborg Castle, when labor crews gathered after work to grab dinner before heading home.

Over time, the action-packed venue grew into Ghana's largest night market with more than 100 vendors serving up mouthwatering Ghanaian staples within a labyrinth of fluorescent-lit stalls.

Don't miss *domedo,* a traditional pork chop, or *kelewele,* a spicy fried plantain served with peanuts. *Banku,* a national dish of plump and fermented dumplings, and the hearty corn-based dough ball, *kenkey,* deserve a taste too. If spice isn't your thing, chomp carefully, says local Ghanaian guide Elvis Wallace-Bruce. Chefs in Ghana love their heat, and many dishes have a spicy sauce of ginger and hot peppers, called *shitor* (pronounced SHEET-o), that promises a kick. If you're sensitive to spice, beware.

Food may be the main attraction, but it's not the only thing on sale at the Osu Night Market. "You can get virtually everything you need here: food, drinks, groceries, and nearby pubs sell liquor and play music," says Wallace-Bruce. Many craftspeople have stalls within the market area as well, and there is a vibrant energy worth experiencing even if you don't buy a thing.

OPPOSITE: Vendors throughout the Osu Night Market grill and sell delicious local cuisine.

NOCTURNAL SAFARI

Explore Zambia's wildlife when it is most active: after dark.

BUDGET: $$$–$$$$$ **WHEN TO GO:** May–October   **ACTIVITY LEVEL:** Intermediate   **GO FOR:** Wildlife

Like clockwork, the sinking sun sets off a flurry of activity across Africa's savannas and woodlands. Big cats and wild dogs hunt, while hyenas tag along for scraps. Nocturnal creatures large and small skitter from their burrows to begin the night's routines. Typically, this hustle and bustle is a safarigoer's lullaby back at base camp, but a night drive takes you into the thick of it. For that, there's no place like Zambia.

Though many national parks throughout Africa restrict after-dark outings, some in Zambia encourage them. Dusk excursions are arranged by safari lodges.

A twilight safari typically begins either immediately following evening sundowners (cocktails and a snack at sunset, usually by your safari vehicle), or after a stop back at the lodge for dinner. Out in the dusky bush, your guide's flashlight will lead your eyes like tunnel vision. The vehicle crawls along as you and your jeep mates listen to the forest sounds and scour the grass and trees for the ultimate clue: two beady eyes glowing back at you. A special membrane behind the retina creates the eerie radiance; it helps animals see at night. Eyeshine hue varies by species, from blue and green to red, white, and yellow.

Like humans, many animals become temporarily blinded by bright white spotlights. It can take up to 30 minutes for their eyes to readjust. This disrupts the animal kingdom's natural nocturnal happenings, from spoiled hunts to injury. Red light, be it a red flashlight or red cellophane covering a spotlight, provides a less obtrusive solution. Many mammals are color-blind and barely

CRITTER CORNER

Megafauna like lions and elephants may wow you on Zambian safaris, but keep an eye out for the dung beetle—a species that uses celestial navigation to survive. Once the beetles roll their ball of doo, they orient themselves by the Milky Way, then use the stars to navigate their meal to safety.

OPPOSITE: **The elusive leopard, found lying on a tree limb at dawn in South Luangwa National Park**

PAGES 28-29: **At dusk, watch as the Luangwa River fills with hundreds of animals, including large herds of elephants.**

notice the hue, if they do at all. That's why Zambian outfitters like Chiawa Safaris solely use red lights on twilight drives.

To experience Zambia's after-dark entertainment, try one of three national parks known for stellar wildlife, cozy accommodations, and pristine, star-decked night skies.

South Luangwa National Park, a remote tangle of woodlands, savanna, acacia shrub, and riverine forest in eastern Zambia, is one of the country's most visited stops. The 3,495 square miles (9,050 km^2) of park sit along one of Africa's longest intact river systems, the Luangwa River. Four of the big five African safari animals—lions, elephants, buffalo, and leopards—call this wilderness home. Other creatures, such as spotted hyenas, wild dogs, genets, civets, and the Pel's fishing owl, may delight safarigoers on after-dark drives too. By day, don't miss a South Luangwa walking safari, one of the park's most famed attractions. This sunlit adventure provides a micro look at the bush. You scan the forest floor for paw prints, identify plants and droppings, and learn about the ecosystem's unsung heroes,

FAST FACT

In 2011, Zambia became one of five southern African countries to join the Kavango-Zambezi Transfrontier Conservation Area (KAZA), home to roughly half of Africa's endangered elephant population. KAZA removed many international border fences to support animal migration routes. Recent data show KAZA's once dwindling elephant population is slowly stabilizing.

such as dung beetles, while single-file following your armed guide—ears perked and binoculars at the ready.

Zambia's oldest and largest national park is Kafue, which covers 8,649 square miles (22,400 km²) just two hours from the city of Livingstone. Kafue promises another captivating night with big potential for big cat sightings—and it's one of only a few Zambian spots to see a cheetah. Rare nocturnal creatures that inhabit this patchwork of plains, river, woodlands, and wetlands include aardvarks, pangolins, bush babies, and honey badgers.

In the 1,580-square-mile (4,092 km²) Lower Zambezi National Park, near the Zambezi River and the Zambia-Zimbabwe border, prepare to have your mind blown by the local megafauna. Massive herds of elephants amble along the riverbanks, then cross from island to island. Predators like lions, leopards, and wild dogs use the inky skies as cover while they stalk prey.

INDIGENOUS STARGAZING

Admire the cosmos with the Mier and ‡Khomani San communities.

BUDGET: $$$ **WHEN TO GO:** Year-round   **ACTIVITY LEVEL:** Mild   **GO FOR:** Stargazing

Stars are links to the past, and few places solidify that connection like the 148,260-acre (60,000 ha) !Ae!Hai Kalahari Heritage Park in South Africa. A Dark Sky Sanctuary, certified by international light pollution authority DarkSky, the park is jointly managed by South African National Parks and the Indigenous Mier and ‡Khomani San communities. The latter descend from the San people, some of Africa's earliest hunter-gatherers. A visit directly supports these communities, while gifting travelers the unique chance to hear astronomical stories passed down through generations.

The San people, which includes several Indigenous groups, have lived across southern Africa for at least 20,000 years and are direct descendants of the first *Homo sapiens*. The savvy hunters spent millennia following game migrations from the mountains to the sea. San people had a spiritual connection to the night sky and created legends surrounding the constellations and cosmic marvels. Take the Milky Way, for example: San legend says a young girl tossed sizzling embers into the sky in the form of a shimmering band to help hunters find their way home.

You can hear more San star stories and learn about their culture from their ‡Khomani San descendants and the Mier community while visiting !Ae!Hai Kalahari Heritage Park, located in the southern stretch of the international

ASTRONOMICAL WONDERS

Rock art contains some of humankind's earliest astronomical recordings. The San people etched space sightings into stone in what is today's South Africa. This art depicts interstellar marvels, such as eclipses, as well as the San culture's beliefs about them. Admire the ancient astronomy with rock art tours in the Drakensberg and Kamberg areas.

OPPOSITE: The stars shine bright above Kgalagadi Transfrontier Park.

PAGES 34-35: A rare sighting: a pair of male African lions at sunrise in South Africa's Kalahari Desert

Kgalagadi Transfrontier Park, which stretches from South Africa into Botswana.

Beneath the hot daytime sun, your trip to this Kalahari Desert park includes hiking among grassy sand dunes, bird-watching, and safari drives to admire giraffes, zebras, and eland. Sun-dappled landscapes are mere appetizers for the star-studded twilight entertainment in store.

By night, you'll take part in interstellar sightseeing. Peek through telescopes and watch laser-guided constellation tours as your Indigenous guide recounts ancestral stories. The sheer darkness (thanks to low light pollution) makes deep space objects, such as nebulae (massive clouds of gas and dust) and the Magellanic Clouds (two of the closest galaxies) visible.

The park's main accommodation, !Xaus Lodge, provides upscale overnights. It's the best spot to post up and enjoy the protected DarkSky-certified nightscapes, which are almost as dark as they were when the first San people called this region home.

The park is more than an astrotourist's dream. It's a case study in the interconnectedness between dark skies and natural ecosystems. Given the Kalahari's high desert heat, which spikes well above 100°F (37.7°C), many animals here are—or have evolved to become—nocturnal. Their survival relies on naturally inky skies. That's why protecting the !Ae!Hai Kalahari Heritage Park's darkness is a win for everyone: the environment, community, and star-loving travelers.

NAMIBRAND NIGHTSCAPES

Look up into some of Africa's darkest skies.

BUDGET: $$$$–$$$$$ **WHEN TO GO:** Year-round   **ACTIVITY LEVEL:** Mild to strenuous   **GO FOR:** Stargazing

Nights are humbling in Namibia's dune-dotted NamibRand Nature Reserve. This private conservation area is an extension of the 55-million-year-old Namib Desert, which stretches from the Atlantic Ocean into southern Africa. More than 60 miles (97 km) separate NamibRand from the nearest communities and, therefore, from the nearest source of light pollution. The result: an evening spectacular where sunset's watercolor skies ready the stage for a real-life planetarium.

In 2012, light pollution authority DarkSky certified NamibRand's skies as some of the darkest in Africa. On the Bortle scale of light pollution—Class 1 being unspoiled black nightscapes, Classes 8 to 9 being New York City's artificial light–drenched Times Square—NamibRand measures in around a 1. This helped it nab DarkSky's coveted Gold Tier International Dark Sky Reserve designation, not to mention a top spot on astrotourism bucket lists.

Stargazing is the main attraction in the 494,000-acre (200,000 ha) nature reserve, which protects a palette of red dunes, gravel plains, and dusky purple mountains. Guides and lodges run an assortment of experiences here, from posh and pampered skygazing to desert treks with open-air sleeps beneath the stars.

Tour operator andBeyond, which runs 30 accommodations across Africa, hosts personalized astronomy experiences at its hip Sossusvlei Lodge,

OTHER MARVELS

NamibRand Nature Reserve's expanse of mysterious fairy circles entices nature lovers. The creation of these circles of grass-barren land, best viewed via hot-air balloon, has puzzled scientists for decades. Origin theories range from meteors to poisonous fungi, but the truth remains unclear.

OPPOSITE: Stars vibrantly dot the sky above the dunes of the Namib Desert.

PAGES 38-39: A dazzle of zebras gallop across the mysterious fairy circles in the NamibRand Nature Reserve.

where 10 stone and glass suites overlook a sea of copper gravel and distant Nubib Mountain peaks. Every evening, a resident astronomer spins guests through the cosmos, with a laser pointer and state-of-the-art telescope to highlight the constellations, distant galaxies, and neighboring planets. A stargazing skylight above each bed keeps the astro entertainment running all night.

Set atop an 820-foot-tall (250 m) dune, safari outfitter Wolwedans Dune Camp offers you a front-row seat to NamibRand Nature Reserve's natural evening entertainment. The tented rooms, tucked among sand and shrubs, share a firepit where guests admire the nightscapes before and after dinner.

For an adventurous trip to the reserve, join a multiday backpacking jaunt with Namibian company Tok Tokkie Trails. A two-night trek across 14 desert miles (22.5 km) takes you through one of the most isolated sides of the reserve. The expedition, with four to six hours of hiking a day, ends with nights camping beneath the stars—and a courtesy welcome concert from nocturnal critters.

Stargazing put NamibRand Nature Reserve on the astrotourism map, but the southern Africa locale inspires by daytime too. Choose from hiking, hot-air balloon rides, and safari excursions. Numerous species inhabit this topographical retreat, including leopards, oryx, springboks, hyenas, and Namibia's endemic dune larks.

NIGHT DIVE

Swim beneath the stars among Lake Malawi's biodiverse marvels.

BUDGET: $$ WHEN TO GO: September–December   ACTIVITY LEVEL: Intermediate   GO FOR: Wildlife

Don't let the term "lake" fool you. At 11,390 square miles (29,500 km²), cerulean Lake Malawi—located between Malawi, Tanzania, and Mozambique—looks more like an ocean. The fish-packed freshwater basin is among the world's most biodiverse lakes. It holds, at minimum, 1,000 fish species, although scientists estimate there could be double that. In certain areas, the lake reaches more than 2,300 feet (700 m) deep—a dusky depth classified as the twilight zone in oceans.

Night diving is a golden ticket to the freshwater action. "It's the only time to see the dolphin fish hunt the cichlids Lake Malawi is famous for," says Debra Van Asche, owner of Nkhata Bay–based Aqua Africa, which runs twilight scuba dives on the lake. The periwinkle dolphinfish don't mind the help from night divers' flashlights as they dart between the lake's gigantic boulders and cliffs in pursuit of their two-inch (5 cm) prey, the cichlids.

These tiny fish, locally known as *mbuna*, are evolutionary wonders. In Lake Malawi, this family of bony freshwater fish has evolved from one to at least 800 species over the past 750,000 years—a feat scientists compare to Darwin's finches in the Galápagos. Visit from September to December, cichlid mating season, for an eye-popping scene. Males dig nests, then attract females via fin-shaking jigs. The females lay eggs, males fertilize them, then the mothers-to-be carry the bundles in their mouths until they hatch.

Water temperatures fluctuate little from day to dusk, remaining between roughly 75 to 84°F (24–29°C). An open water certification from the Professional Association of Diving Instructors (PADI), or equivalent training, is required.

OPPOSITE: Explore the wonders of Lake Malawi that only emerge under the water at night.

BWITI CEREMONY

Learn about Gabonese spirituality in a traditional village community.

BUDGET: $$$$–$$$$$ **WHEN TO GO:** Year-round   **ACTIVITY LEVEL:** Mild   **GO FOR:** Culture

G abon intrigues intrepid travelers with less trodden safari circuits and the chance to spot "surfing" hippos that ride waves off Loango National Park's coast. But one of the West African country's most enriching experiences is the Bwiti rituals, which take place within the villages of the Punu, Mitsogo, and Fang people from dusk to dawn.

In the 19th century, missionaries descended upon Gabon hoping to spread Christianity and eradicate Indigenous beliefs. The Mitsogo people of southern Gabon fled to the jungle, where they met the Babongo Pygmy community and were educated in the use of the psychedelic iboga plant, a powerful and long-lasting hallucinogen. This knowledge sharing formalized the Bwiti belief system, or religion, which relies heavily on the plant's spiritual power.

During traditional twilight ceremonies, members of the Bwiti spiritual discipline summon spirits and commune with their ancestors. It's a night of polyrhythmic music, choreographed dance, and colorful costumes, with the transcendent power of the iboga plant's root bark at the ceremony's core.

Authentic cultural hubs like Ndossi Village, a community in Akanda National Park, welcome visitors to learn about their traditions, including the history of these ancestral ceremonies, which date back to the late 1800s. Guests are welcome to attend the ritual as bystanders, but you cannot ingest the plant unless you have completed lengthy spiritual work beforehand. To coordinate a Bwiti ceremony visit, hire Gabonese tour operators, such as African Trotteur.

OPPOSITE: During the Bwiti rituals, dancers dress in skirts, headbands, jewelry, and leaves and cover their bodies in white chalk and a special red paste.

FELUCCA CAMPING

Sail and snooze your way down the Nile to explore its treasures.

BUDGET: $$-$$$ **WHEN TO GO:** October–April   **ACTIVITY LEVEL:** Intermediate   **GO FOR:** Culture

Stars twinkle overhead as moonlight-swaddled temples glimmer in the distance. Soon, the echoing call to prayer will stir you awake for another sherbet-colored Egyptian sunrise along one of Earth's longest and most famed rivers.

Many travelers dream about sailing the Nile River. Taking the trip on a traditional felucca sailboat only adds to the adventure. "You're closer to the rhythms of the Nile," says Alexandra Baackes, founder of Alex in Wanderland and Wander Women Retreats, who's traveled the Nile by felucca three times. "You watch it wake up and fall asleep."

The wooden sailboats are icons of the more than 4,100-mile-long (6,600 km) Nile. Egyptians revolutionized transportation when they shifted from small reed boats to the larger and sturdier single-sailed feluccas, which bolstered trade along this north-flowing waterway. It's unknown exactly when Egyptians constructed the first felucca, but historians believe they've filled the Nile for centuries, possibly as far back as the Middle Ages.

Today, the hand-stitched lateen sails still dot the Nile up and down its length. Half-day felucca trips are Egypt tourist staples, particularly around golden hour (sunset or sunrise). But those who are eager for a truly intrepid adventure can float down the Nile via felucca on a two- or three-day guided journey. The most popular camping itineraries by felucca run from Aswan,

ASTRONOMICAL WONDERS

As you watch the night sky from your Nile felucca, know that perhaps even Cleopatra and King Tut admired these same nightscapes. Ancient Egyptians built pyramids and temples facing north due to their belief that pharaohs became stars in the northern sky in the afterlife.

OPPOSITE: Feluccas have been used to sail the Nile River for centuries.

PAGES 46-47: Off your vessel, explore ancient Egyptian sites like the Karnak temple complex, a mix of pillars and temples along with other buildings, near Luxor.

an ancient city and the gateway to the rock-carved Abu Simbel temple complex, to Luxor, an open-air museum known as ancient Thebes, with temples, monuments, and the Valley of the Kings royal burial grounds, the final resting place of King Tut.

Sightseeing bookends the expedition, but once you're out on the boat, the river is the main attraction. "This is really a case of the journey being the destination," says Baackes. "It's about connecting to the history and nature of Egypt, rather than basking in the luxury of it."

Unlike a traditional Nile sightseeing cruise, felucca sailing is about relaxing and lazing. During the day, you'll swim in the river, sunbathe on the deck, and watch as myriad temples and monuments roll by. As night hits, your sailing team docks on the bank so guests can disembark, stroll, or even wade in for an evening soak. Traditional Egyptian fare, such as *ful* (fava bean stew) and Nile perch, will fill your belly, while starlit skies, music, and dancing satiate your soul.

Sleeping arrangements depend on the vessel. Many passengers snooze in a sleeping bag, or beneath blankets, on an oversize main-deck bed. "It's a sleepover vibe," says Baackes. "We all sleep, eat, and laze together on one big mattress."

In addition to scenic splendor, felucca sailing provides a sustainable Nile cruise option, as most of the boats remain wind powered.

UGANDA
NIGHT FISHING
Cast a line under starry skies.

BUDGET: $$$–$$$$ **WHEN TO GO:** October–March   **ACTIVITY LEVEL:** Intermediate   **GO FOR:** Adventure

There's angling, then there's angling under the moonlight on one of the world's largest lakes. If the latter sounds like it's right up your alley, find your way to Jinja, a Ugandan town near the northern shores of Lake Victoria.

The idea of night fishing is hardly new here. For decades, regional fishers have hit the water with paraffin (and, increasingly, solar-powered) angling lamps. They fasten the lights onto rafts of tethered dry reeds to entice the small silver cyprinid fish, which travel toward the surface after dusk. The sardine-like animal is indigenous to the lake. It's one of the most reliable fishing options remaining since the invasive Nile perch wiped out hundreds of species after it was introduced to the lake in the mid-1950s. Commercial anglers glide out beneath shifting orange-to-indigo skies to set their lamps and nets, then sell their fresh hauls the next morning.

Though this traditional experience is largely reserved for locals—it's their livelihood—Jinja offers numerous after-dark sportfishing trips. A nighttime outing lets you cast beneath constellations as calls from crickets, birds, and distant animals bounce across the forest-flanked lake.

Trips run near the source of the Nile, where Lake Victoria meets the famed river. During trips, which run from 7 p.m. to 12 a.m., you might catch tilapia, Nile perch, or silver cyprinid. After-hours fishing requires a special guide for safety, as well as to coordinate logistics and permits. Avoid the full moon for best conditions; research suggests fish are less active around this time.

OPPOSITE: Fishermen set their nets in Lake Victoria, with only a lamp to light their nightly efforts.

PART TWO

ASIA

Spend a night camped out under the stars on the Great Wall of China, one of the New Seven Wonders of the World (page 52).

GREAT WALL CAMPING

Sleep in a centuries-old watchtower on China's greatest world wonder.

BUDGET: $$-$$$ **WHEN TO GO:** April–May or September–October
ACTIVITY LEVEL: Intermediate   **GO FOR:** Adventure

Around 220 B.C., Chinese emperor Qin Shi Huang set in motion one of humankind's most ambitious architectural feats: the Great Wall of China. It took more than 2,000 years and numerous dynasties to construct the colossus, which zigzags across the country's mountainous northern border for up to 3,400 miles (5,500 km). Today the Great Wall is known as one of the New Seven Wonders of the World and is listed as a UNESCO World Heritage site.

Despite the name, the structure is less of a wall and more of a fortification tool. Its barriers, fortresses, barracks, and watchtowers were all designed to fend off nomadic invaders. Soldiers perched in watchtowers to monitor enemy activity and lit torches to alert troops.

Today, most visits to the Great Wall include a stop in one, or several, of these watchtowers. Yet the ultimate experience, one few get a chance to have, is camping overnight in a watchtower.

At night on this high, powerful post, "you feel as if you can touch the stars," says Terrence Ou, CEO of Great Wall Adventure Club, which runs private and group camping trips in select sections of the historic structure. The excursions begin with guided daytime hikes up and down secluded, and often strenuous, stretches of the wall. Treks range from around four to 10 or more hours, depending on the route.

OTHER MARVELS

China's isn't the universe's largest great wall. The Hercules-Corona Borealis Great Wall is a supercluster (a large group of smaller galaxies) so enormous it defies all logic. It's 10 billion light-years wide—roughly 10 percent of the diameter of the observable universe.

OPPOSITE: This isn't glamping: Camping on the Great Wall requires a tent and hauling your own provisions.

PAGES 54-55: The most preserved section of the wall runs 5,500 miles (8,850 km) east to west and dates back to the Ming dynasty.

As the sun descends, hikers gather to admire the sea of rolling peaks bathed in amber and gold light. Then, they refuel with a hike down and off the wall to a mom-and-pop restaurant in town. With headlamps lit, trekkers clamber back up to the night's watchtower to help the guides set up camp (tents and sleeping bags), and admire the remote sky's panorama of planets and constellations, as well as the glimmering Milky Way.

These nightscapes have intrigued Chinese scientists since at least the fourth century. The country's astronomers were the first to reliably record a total solar eclipse, in 780 B.C. You can learn more about the local astronomical history and ancient Chinese constellations via the 500-year-old Beijing Ancient Observatory before your camping trip.

The Great Wall, reached via Beijing, is divided into sections. Guided camping trips run in three main areas. Numerous ancient battles occurred on the Gubeikou stretch, 75 miles (120 km) from Beijing. The wild, unkempt expanse of wall, flanked by scraggly brush and distant jagged peaks, features more than 100 watchtowers.

WHILE YOU'RE THERE

Camping is just one of the Great Wall's unique experiences. For another adventure, try tobogganing. The wall's popular Mutianyu section, located roughly 40 miles (65 km) north of Beijing, runs a cable car to funnel visitors up and down the wall, with an optional five-minute toboggan slide down. The thrilling run spans one mile (1.6 km), with in-car controls for acceleration and braking.

ABOVE: Experience the wall like an ancient soldier from one of its watchtowers. Historians estimate the wall originally had nearly 25,000 towers.

OPPOSITE: Guided tours of the wall provide opportunities to hear the history of this ancient fortress—and help with setting up camp for the night.

Huanghuacheng, known for its steep stairs and breathtaking vistas across lakes and emerald-bearded peaks, is another portion that allows watchtower sleeps. Construction on this stretch of fortification, which protects the nearby Ming Tombs, a collection of mausoleums from the Ming dynasty, took nearly 200 years. Huanghuacheng lies 47 miles (75 km) north of Beijing.

The vertiginous Jiankou expanse, 50 miles (80 km) north of Beijing, provides a quiet camping night—but you'll have to work for it. Jiankou is one of the most dangerous parts of the Great Wall—its steep, rugged fortress is built directly into a jagged mountain ridge.

Millennia of natural wear, tear, and battles have destroyed much of the Great Wall. To protect the wall and travelers, hikers must hire a registered guiding service, such as Great Wall Adventure Club, to overnight on the world wonder.

TAI HANG FIRE DRAGON DANCE

Watch a sparkly creature slink through the streets of Hong Kong.

BUDGET: $ **WHEN TO GO:** September–October   **ACTIVITY LEVEL:** Mild   **GO FOR:** Culture

Smoke from incense cloaks the streets. A steady drumbeat builds anticipation. Spectators pack roads and alleyways, each angling for a glimpse of what may soon round the corner: a 220-foot (67 m) dragon snaking its way through Tai Hang, Hong Kong.

This is the Tai Hang Fire Dragon Dance, a century-old tradition that fills its namesake neighborhood with buzzing energy, cultural pride, and celebrators from across the globe. Yet despite its exuberant present, the dragon dance has a somber past. In the late 1800s, a fatal plague swept through the humble fishing village of Tai Hang, killing many residents. An elder of the village had a dream in which Buddha advised him to perform a firecracker-adorned dragon dance during China's Mid-Autumn Festival to end the plight. It worked. And the residents of Tai Hang, now a hip neighborhood just south of Hong Kong Island's Causeway Bay, have been performing the Fire Dragon Dance ever since.

The star of the parade is the gigantic handcrafted dragon—a spectacle that takes at least one month to construct. It's made with a sequence of 32 serpentine segments packed with straw and more than 12,000 twinkling incense sticks, plus a 110-pound (50 kg) head. The artisan team behind the creature binds pearl straw around hemp rope and rattan to create the dragon's body.

BEST BITE

No Mid-Autumn Festival is complete without mooncakes, the holiday's quintessential treat. These round pastries are typically stuffed with sesame, red bean, or lotus pastes, and sometimes with whole salted egg yolks at their center. The delicacy has been part of festival merriment for millennia.

OPPOSITE: The dragon at the Tai Hang Fire Dragon Dance is decorated with more than 12,000 burning incense sticks and carried by 300 people.

PAGES 60-61: A drummer leads the blazing, dancing dragon through the streets.

The event begins at dusk and lasts around two hours. A group of 300 dancers performs for three nights, toting the dragon through the streets and dancing to live music along the way.

The dragon's annual debut coincides with the start of the countrywide Mid-Autumn Festival, one of China's most important holidays. The festival is an ode to the fall harvest and a time for families to join together in prayer for the future. The Fire Dragon Dance runs from the beginning of the festival until the full moon (usually the 15th day of the eighth month of the Chinese calendar, or somewhere between September and October on the Gregorian calendar).

The best vantage point is on Wun Sha Street, says Cheung Kwok Ho, Almon, acting commander in chief of the Tai Hang Fire Dragon Dance. "The dragon passes through this street with its dragon head facing the crowd." The festivities finish here, and the dragon carriers gift remaining incense to the Wun Sha Street crowds.

To learn more about the tradition, and the intricate dragon-crafting process passed down through generations, spend a day at the Tai Hang Fire Dragon Heritage Centre, located at 12 School Street. The facility includes the history of the dance and Tai Hang's Indigenous Hakka culture, as well as a themed restaurant to enjoy a fusion of Hakka and modern fare.

MIDNIGHT MARKETS

Indulge in a sampler of late-night snacks through the streets of Taiwan.

BUDGET: $ **WHEN TO GO:** Year-round   **ACTIVITY LEVEL:** Mild   **GO FOR:** Local bites

S izzling sausage, crackling omelets, hits of nose-startling tofu—this is just a sampler of the sounds, smells, and tastes primed to jostle your senses throughout Taiwan's night markets.

These energetic Taiwanese hangouts actually stem from mainland China: After the Chinese Civil War of the 1940s, defeated Kuomintang Army troops and millions of Chinese citizens, including some of the country's most celebrated chefs, retreated to Taiwan. They brought with them delectable recipes that they began to sell near main gathering places.

"Usually, night markets will have a historic temple in or right next to it," says Mini Kao, who grew up next to the Raohe Night Market in Taiwan. "People go to the temples like their community centers; that's how the vendors and food stalls first started." Today, more than 100 of these bustling twilight thoroughfares fill the island, with vendors selling *xiaochi,* the Chinese word for snack, to hungry locals and visitors alike.

To hit as many Taiwanese night markets as possible, head to the capital city, Taipei. The buzzing metropolis has more than 30 market outposts, each with its own signature dish. Even better? You can sample stinky tofu, an odorous, but delicious, fermented bean curd considered the island's national snack, at nearly every one.

Shilin Night Market, one of the capital's oldest and largest after-dark hubs,

OPPOSITE: **The Raohe Night Market in Taipei's Song-shan District is a lively scene after nightfall.**

PAGES 64-65: **At the Shilin Night Market in Taipei, a vendor makes oyster omelets for hungry patrons.**

provides a maze of 500 food stalls with an underground Shilin Night Market Food Court. It runs from late afternoon into the wee hours of the morning. Given its popularity, stalls and food stations have expanded into the streets and alleyways surrounding the main market, with vendors selling not just xiaochi, but fashion, art, and souvenirs. Come late to enjoy the tradition's signature bright lights and gregarious crowds, but prepare to arrive early if you crave the market's signature oyster omelet. This Shilin icon, an egg omelet stuffed with oysters and topped with a savory, slightly spicy, sauce, sells out quickly.

Another Taipei must-see, the Raohe Night Market begins at the ornate and dragon-decked Ciyou Temple, which soars above the food stalls at six stories tall. Raohe is best known for its Fuzhou black pepper bun. To try this crispy pork bun splashed with a juicy black pepper sauce and topped with onions, prepare to queue up. The Raohe Night Market opens in the afternoon, with its peak activity hitting at dinnertime. It stays open until around 11 p.m., with hundreds of cheery vendors vying for your appetite.

WHERE TO STAY

Have a grand night at Taipei's 14-floor Grand Hotel, which was built in 1952 and is adorned with more than 200,000 dragons. The hotel has welcomed world-renowned guests like Dwight D. Eisenhower, Nelson Mandela, Margaret Thatcher, and Ronald Reagan. It's within walking distance of Shilin Night Market.

TAZAUNGDAING LIGHTS FESTIVAL

Spend a night of revelry with fire balloons and a human-powered Ferris wheel.

BUDGET: $ WHEN TO GO: November   ACTIVITY LEVEL: Mild   GO FOR: Culture

The end of rainy season is cause for celebration across Myanmar, and the mountainous Shan State capital, Taunggyi, takes its debauchery seriously. Think a human-powered Ferris wheel, fireworks, tattoo stations, carnival games, and the most eye-popping attraction of all, a nightly fire balloon competition. It's all part of the country's Tazaungdaing Festival, known as the Festival of Lights. The week of merriment occurs annually around the full moon of Tazaungmon, the eighth month of the traditional Myanmar calendar (typically November).

Though cities throughout Myanmar run their own Tazaungdaing Festivals, few make as big a splash as Taunggyi. Its one-week observance turns the city into a circus, drawing hundreds of thousands of attendees with one-of-a-kind spectacles. The fire balloon competition, considered the main event, is not your average hot-air balloon show.

For months, local teams concoct dazzling balloons made of paper; many reach up to 30 feet (9 m) tall. Participants debut their works of art each night of the festival, with a new launch roughly every 30 minutes.

The rollout of each balloon is an extravaganza in and of itself. There's the procession, where teammates blare music atop cars while toting their enormous balloon through the crowds. Next comes inflation via fire sticks, and the launch, where dozens of attached candles twinkle as the paper orb rises.

OTHER MARVELS

On the nights before and of the Tazaung-mon full moon, competitors weave from dusk to dawn to create the longest, most intricate *matho thingan*, a sacred yellow monk robe.

OPPOSITE: Participants at the Tazaungdaing Lights Festival send their paper balloons soaring each night to a chorus of cheers.

PAGES 68-69: Monks and Buddhist devotees light candles on the steps of pagodas and temples during the full-moon celebration.

Each group's moment in the spotlight ends with a grand finale: The balloon base erupts with firecrackers. Then it's time for the next team to start, then the next one. "There's nothing else like it out there," says Dustin Main, author of *This Myanmar Life*, a decade-long documentary photography project about the country.

From haphazard fireworks to potential balloon crashes, safety is a major concern at the festival. "Having a local guide with you who knows what's going on is a must," says Main. "Be aware of the wind, and never be under the path of a balloon, no matter how high it is."

For another thrill, don't miss the human-powered Ferris wheel, where ride workers spin your vessel like a wheel on a game show. See Taunggyi's streets come to life as celebrators tote glowing lotus flowers and lantern-decked floats before the nightly balloon launches begin.

The Tazaungdaing Festival is also a great time to taste Shan dishes, such as *hin-htoke*, a blend of spring onion and rice flour steamed in a banana leaf and drizzled with garlic oil on top. According to Main, "it's what dreams are made of."

TRAVEL TIP

Following a 2021 coup in Myanmar, the U.S. Department of State issued a Level 4 (do not travel) advisory for the country due to armed conflict and civil unrest. Stay up to date on the latest via *travel.state.gov,* and learn how to help those displaced by the violence via the United Nations Refugee Agency.

SINGAPORE

SINGING TREES

Take in a nightly spectacle of sound, light, and color in the Gardens by the Bay.

BUDGET: $ WHEN TO GO: Year-round   ACTIVITY LEVEL: Mild   GO FOR: Nature

A visit to Singapore's fantastical Gardens by the Bay feels like stepping onto the set of *Avatar*. To go deeper into this real-life Pandora, visit at night, when the wondrous, high-tech trees erupt in kaleidoscopic hues and tunes.

You can watch the display throughout the Supertree Grove, a collection of glowing trees that tower up to 164 feet (50 m). True to the destination's futuristic theming, this isn't your average flora. Vertical gardens adorn these tree-shaped structures, which are made of concrete and steel. The patch of trees collectively grows 162,000 plants from 200 plant species, including orchids and ferns. Nearly half of the structures also harvest solar energy. It's part of the garden's push to educate visitors about the world's ecosystems and the innovative sustainability solutions available to us.

During the twice-a-night show, each roughly 15 minutes long, the horticultural haven's innovative grove illuminates to the beat of a curated soundtrack. Garden Rhapsody's evening set lists vary by season. There's opera, waltz, disco, classical music, and pop culture favorites like *Star Wars* nights. The trees radiate and flicker as beats drop during the free show.

For the best vantage point, snag a seat on the lawn, and come early to tour the facility's Flower Dome, a colossal growing center that set the Guinness World Record for the largest glass greenhouse in 2015.

OPPOSITE: **In the Supertree Grove at Gardens by the Bay, 12 of the structures stand between 82 and 164 feet (25–50 m) tall and are covered in a variety of plants, including orchids, ferns, and tropical climbers.**

FIREFLY KAYAKING

Paddle through the Bohol island mangroves as the sky twinkles with fireflies.

BUDGET: $$ **WHEN TO GO:** Year-round **ACTIVITY LEVEL:** Intermediate **GO FOR:** Nature

A magic show awaits in the Abatan River's dense mangrove maze. The main act: a flurry of sparkling *Pteroptyx macdermotti* fireflies, a species that's endemic to the Philippines and the forested waterway on the island of Bohol.

These insects are among the rarest fireflies on Earth, and like many creatures, they face threats from human interference, such as light pollution, habitat loss, and ecosystem erosion from motorboats. Local outfitter KayakAsia Philippines uses its firefly paddle tours to help travelers witness and learn about the bioluminescent beetles in a quiet, low-impact way, and in hopes it inspires efforts to protect these insects.

The two-hour outing starts at the river mouth just before sunset. You'll marvel at golden hour's purple-pink skies before gliding deep into the river's inner channels, where dozens of thick mangrove species protect the fireflies and the wetland ecosystem. "The whole trip aims to give a better understanding of how hectares upon hectares of mangrove wetland are actually an interconnected corridor for ecosystems to thrive," says KayakAsia Philippines co-founder Rey Marcelo Donaire.

Paddlers glide from tree to tree to admire swarms of the sparkling insects, which synchronously flicker to communicate via neon green flashes. Meanwhile, guides keep watch for signs of illegal and destructive activities, such as harvesting mangrove trees for timber. "Each tree is too important to lose," says Donaire, noting these mangroves do more than protect animals; they also keep enormous amounts of carbon dioxide out of our atmosphere.

OPPOSITE: The simultaneous glow from fireflies lights the trees along the Abatan River, almost like a holiday light show.

SPARKLING SQUID

Experience the springtime arrival of glow-in-the-dark cephalopods in Toyama Bay.

BUDGET: $ **WHEN TO GO:** April **ACTIVITY LEVEL:** Mild **GO FOR:** Wildlife

You don't have to go into orbit to find aliens. They're right here on Earth in Japan's Toyama Bay. Every spring, millions of electric blue squid hit the sea surface for their annual spawning—a display that is, frankly, otherworldly.

These ocean dwellers may not technically count as aliens, but given their rare sightings and surreal glow, they're as close as we might get on planet Earth. Known in Japan as *hotaru-ika,* the three-inch (7 cm) cephalopods live 1,200 feet (365 m) below the sea surface. The females typically rise to the bay's surface from about late March to May when the current drops them here to complete their one-year life cycles by spawning. It's a spectacle that draws thousands of onlookers every year.

Bioluminescence is the star of this teal light show, which creates a ripple of constellations on the ocean surface. Unlike fireflies, which use the chemical reaction of bioluminescence to produce light in their bellies, Japan's cephalopods have light-producing organs known as photophores, which generate a cerulean glow across their bodies and tentacles.

And these squid don't just shimmer; they flash in unison, or in a series of patterns. Scientists haven't confirmed the purpose, but some believe the bursts of color may help them communicate or fend off predators.

To see this light show for yourself, join a firefly squid boat tour. Trips depart around 2:30 a.m. from Wave Park Namerikawa near the Hotaruika Museum, a venue dedicated to the species. Out on the bay, beneath pitch-black skies, the inky ocean twinkles as millions of the neon blue creatures shimmer near

OPPOSITE: Firefly squid typically live in the deep sea, where their ability to produce light, a type of countershading, protects them from predators.

PAGES 76-77: The shores of Toyama Bay glow blue as squid wash ashore during this annual event.

the surface. This spawning scene marks the end of the female firefly squid's life. In their final minutes, the squid release their fertilized eggs. Anglers use nets to scoop up the shiny squid, which are often served as sashimi across Japan; the eggs are tiny enough to slip through the nets.

Trips to see the firefly squid typically require an offshore boat ride (available only when the seas are calm). Some years, when the moon and tides are just right, the glitzy squid can even wash up on the coast, bejeweling the Toyama Bay shoreline with a blanket of bright blue cephalopods.

To learn about the creatures before you hit the water, visit the Hotaruika Museum, located in Namerikawa City on the shore of Toyama Bay. The museum is open from 9 a.m. to 5 p.m. and features an exhibition hall and immersive live theater light shows to explain the famous squid and other local bioluminescent critters, like plankton.

OTHER MARVELS

Glowing squid are just one of Japan's after-dark enchantments. A four-hour boat ride from Tokyo drops you on Kozushima, one of the world's few Dark Sky Islands, certified by light pollution authority DarkSky. After just one year with reduced light pollution, Kozushima's nesting green sea turtles returned, which scientists say could be attributed to the island's push to protect its night skies.

LANTERN RELEASES

Celebrate Thailand's annual Yi Peng and Loy Krathong festivals.

BUDGET: $ **WHEN TO GO:** November   **ACTIVITY LEVEL:** Mild   **GO FOR:** Culture

Every November during the full moon, thousands of sparkling lanterns drift through the sky above Thailand, and nearly as many twinkling floats dot the country's waterways. It's the culmination of two major holidays: the Yi Peng lantern festival and Loy Krathong.

Yi Peng is the best known of the two festivals. The three-day holiday draws visitors from around the world. Celebrators gather to release lanterns, called *khom loi,* into the dark sky, filling it with warm, gold-hued lights. The holiday is timed to the full moon in November, the 12th month of the Thai lunar calendar, to mark the end of monsoon season and the beginning of lighter days and cooler weather. According to local lore, lanterns that disappear into the darkness symbolize good luck in the coming year. Many celebrators also write messages on their shimmery cylinders to put their wishes out into the universe.

Loy Krathong is an entirely separate festival but held around the same time. The tradition is seen as a way to pay respect to river deities, as well as wash away sins and misdeeds of the past year. During Loy Krathong, merrymakers launch small and large floats, known as *krathongs,* adorned with banana leaves, flowers, and incense sticks into the town's rivers, canals, and lakes. Legend has it that if a couple simultaneously releases floats and the vessels reach the other side of the river in tandem, the two will stay together forever.

BEST BITE

The after-dark market culture is strong in Thailand, starting with the bustling Chiang Mai Night Bazaar. Blocks upon blocks of vendors dish out savory and sweet street food, such as noodle dishes and spring rolls, from 6 p.m. onward. Don't leave without a helping of mango sticky rice.

OPPOSITE: Celebrators release lanterns—symbols of new beginnings and hope for a good year ahead—into the sky.

PAGES 80-81: Hundreds gather to release their lanterns at the Tudong-kasatarn temple.

"It's about making merit, casting away and atoning for the sins of the prior year, and hoping for success and happiness in the year to come," says Jariya "Yaya" Plaikeaw, operations manager and guide for the Tuk Tuk Club in northern Thailand.

Chiang Mai, in northern Thailand, is the best hub to learn about and enjoy both sacred celebrations, but in recent years, local authorities have restricted lantern releases to prevent fires. Now, there are ticketed events with select release nights.

If the lantern-launch crowds of Chiang Mai look daunting, Plaikeaw recommends the nearby town of Mae Hong Son, roughly 150 miles (240 km) away. It's an equally impressive yet more laid-back Yi Peng stop. The town hosts a fair around its temple-lined lake, with lantern releases, traditional dancing, Thai boxing, and food stalls.

Hire a guide to help you navigate the ins and outs of the lantern and float experiences. Or you can join in on your own. Some of the best Chiang Mai perches to watch the Yi Peng and

WHILE YOU'RE THERE

Choose your wildlife travels wisely. Instead of exploitative elephant rides, which hurt the animals, head just outside Chiang Mai to Elephant Nature Park, a safe space for more than 100 elephants rescued from tourist riding, circus shows, and logging. Visitors can watch the gentle giants graze, splash in the river, and roam freely across the park's forested grounds.

ABOVE: Traditionally, Loy Krathong celebrated the end of the rice harvest season by giving thanks to the goddess of water.

OPPOSITE: Krathong lanterns decorated with candles, lotus leaves, incense, and flowers are released on canals, rivers, and other waterways.

Loy Krathong releases include the Ping River and Tha Pae Gate. There are also pricier, ticketed mass-release events like the Chiang Mai CAD Khomloy Sky Lantern Festival. The event is held for two nights and includes a Thai buffet dinner, two lanterns, and one krathong per person, as well as drinks, and a hand-painted keepsake. Whichever way you choose to celebrate, Chiang Mai is bursting with energy. Throughout the city, temples and homes decorate entrances with flowers and coconut leaves, and many streets are lit by candlelight at night.

In recent years, the Thai people have evolved the Yi Peng lantern festival to ensure the released lights are as eco-friendly as possible. If you're joining a launch, aim for natural and decomposable lantern materials instead of plastic. The local government also runs post-event cleanups for both Yi Peng and Loy Krathong.

ELECTRIC BLUE LAVA

Summit the Kawah Ijen volcano overnight to see a turquoise lava flow.

BUDGET: $-$$ **WHEN TO GO:** May–September   **ACTIVITY LEVEL:** Strenuous   **GO FOR:** Adventure

As night blankets Indonesia's island of Java, an otherworldly electric blue ooze seems to spill from towering Kawah Ijen—yet this twilight sight is actually an illusion. The volcano's sapphire flames make the magma itself appear blue. This shocking scene stirs travelers out of their beds well before dawn for a twilight-to-sunrise trek up the active and seemingly jewel-hued volcano.

Of course, there is a scientific explanation behind this otherworldly sight. The blue flames result when the volcano's sulfuric gases react to oxygen in the air. The brilliant teal is only visible at night; by day, the lava in the Kawah Ijen crater looks like any other volcano.

Tours to admire the nighttime spectacular depart from the closest town, Banyuwangi, between midnight and 2 a.m. You'll don a headlamp and clamber up gravel and dirt trails beneath countless bright stars, with a stop to admire the crater's cerulean fire before summiting the 9,085-foot (2,769 m) Kawah Ijen peak for a spectacular sunrise. Depending on conditions, travelers may hike partially down into the crater too.

On the daylit descent, hikers can admire the volcano's turquoise sulfur lake, one of the largest acidic bodies of water in the world. Gas masks are required as you near the top of Kawah Ijen. It's best to climb during the dry season, from May to September. A tour guide is recommended for safety.

OPPOSITE: Kawah Ijen glows blue as the volcano's sulfurous gas meets the air.

INDIA

MONASTERY STARGAZING

Learn Buddhist and Tibetan sky lore in the Indian Himalaya.

BUDGET: $ **WHEN TO GO:** May–September **ACTIVITY LEVEL:** Mild **GO FOR:** Stargazing

Skygazing beneath a dome of stars is awe-inspiring, but a growing astrotourism program in northwest India's mountainous Ladakh region highlights the activity's potential for social change. The initiative, known as Astrostays, helps rural villagers turn their naturally dark skies into empowering and sustainable livelihoods. Since its founding, Astrostays has created six community-led destinations, employed 35 local women, and received more than 1,200 travelers.

The backdrop couldn't be better. Above the Indian Himalaya's snow-crowned fangs, the inky skies erupt with stars, planets, and deep space objects. Villagers who have been trained in astronomy welcome travelers with a blend of science and culture: telescopes, Ladakhi sky lore, hearty fare, and overnight homestays.

By simply visiting and stargazing, astrotourists support economic opportunity among rural Ladakhi communities, particularly women. Since launching in the village of Maan in 2018, Astrostays, a joint partnership between the International Astronomical Union Office of Astronomy for Development and tour outfitter Global Himalayan Expedition (GHE), has generated enough income to fund a community greenhouse and solar water heaters.

In 2022, Astrostays added a one-of-a-kind cosmic perch for travelers: a

ASTRONOMICAL WONDERS

Ladakh's pristine night skies helped it claim India's first DarkSky-certified destination in 2022: the Hanle Dark Sky Reserve. This high-altitude stargazing hub, the site of the Indian Astronomical Observatory, delights astrotourists roughly 160 miles (260 km) south of the Phyang Monastery.

OPPOSITE: Stars streak the sky above an ancient Buddhist monastery in the Himalaya outside Ladakh.

PAGES 88-89: A giant statue of the Maitreya Buddha, or Future Buddha, sits in the Thiksey Monastery in Ladakh.

16th-century Buddhist monastery. The hilltop Phyang Monastery, cushioned on a grassy overlook beneath the region's signature saw-toothed peaks, now welcomes astrotourists for night sky enrichment. The experience centers on the adjacent and entirely female-run Cosmohub, an astronomical gathering space with telescopes, night-sky education, and cultural experiences, including a small market with handicrafts and organic products. Because many Buddhist monks speak to the public sparingly, and sometimes not at all, the monks taught village women their spiritual cosmology and constellations so they, in turn, could share this knowledge with sky-loving travelers.

Most trips to the Phyang Monastery run for three and a half hours. They launch from the main town of Leh, roughly a 30-minute drive away. Upon arrival, you'll tour the centuries-old monastery and admire the frescoes and paintings that illustrate the monks' traditional sky beliefs. Visitors are invited to join a monastery prayer session

WHILE YOU'RE THERE

See the lake of many colors: Pangong Tso, located roughly 90 miles (145 km) from Leh, is a high-altitude landlocked lake that appears blue, green, gold, or pink depending on the sky color. Light refraction at the lake's high altitude of 14,272 feet (4,350 m) contributes to its chameleonic effect. Rocks in the Pangong Tso bed discharge salt, giving the lake a saltwater consistency that attracts migrating birds like Brahminy ducks and black-necked cranes.

ABOVE: Monks blow a *dungchen*, a long trumpet or horn, during a Tibetan Buddhist ceremony.

OPPOSITE: Buddhist prayer flags flap in the wind along a path leading to the Namgyal Tsemo Monastery in Ladakh.

before heading to the Cosmohub's night sky museum, which blends western science with Buddhist and Tibetan cosmology.

After learning about the local culture and cosmos, it's time for the telescopes. "Walking through the museum and monastery and talking about what astronomy means to the people in Ladakh gives travelers a rich flavor when they actually start the stargazing session," says Sonal Asgotraa of GHE, which coordinates monastery trips. The Cosmohub's powerful telescopes explore outer space, offering views of planets, galaxies, nebulae, and star clusters.

True to Ladakhi hospitality traditions, your night sky hosts will ensure you don't leave Cosmohub hungry. Homemade dishes, such as vegetable *thukpa* (a savory soup and noodle dish) and *puli* (Ladakhi cookies), are almost as mind-blowing as the Himalayan nightscapes.

INDIA

DIWALI BY NIGHT

Take in India's largest celebration at its height: after dark.

BUDGET: $-$$$$ **WHEN TO GO:** October–November   **ACTIVITY LEVEL:** Mild   **GO FOR:** Culture

World-renowned Diwali is a celebration of love, light, and happiness. During India's most important holiday, the skies glow with firecrackers and the streets are adorned with rainbow-hued designs (a form of art known as *rangoli,* made of rice, flowers, or dyed powder) and millions of glistening *diya* oil lamps. The tradition is a sacred one—and the largest festival in India. With the right plan and guide, travelers can respectfully join the merriment too.

Diwali marks the victory of light over darkness, which is symbolized with festival icons such as diyas. The holiday occurs around the new moon during the Hindu month of Kartik (October or November, depending on the year). It's celebrated by Hindus, Jains, Sikhs, Buddhists, and many Muslims. Each day of the five-day celebration has a special meaning, and many of the holiday's best known festivities take place after dark.

Most practitioners spend the holiday at home with family, but travelers can partake via a public light show or a special Diwali tour. "It's a magical time to see joy and celebration on such a large scale," says Suman Rathod, a spokesperson for TourRadar, which runs Festival of Lights trips from New Delhi to Jaipur, including traditional feasts, visits to shimmering temples, and a night spent watching fireworks. "The atmosphere is full of love and harmony."

OPPOSITE: The Ganges River fills with thousands of floating *diya* lamps on the night of Kartik Purnima, the most sacred day of Diwali.

PAGES 94-95: *Rangoli* decorations made with flower petals are among the decorations seen along the streets, in homes, and on temple floors during Diwali.

Uttar Pradesh is a can't-miss Diwali destination. In this North Indian state, the shimmery town of Ayodhya reflects off the glassy Ghaghara River, a holy body of water that draws millions of devotees for sacred dips each Diwali. The river wows with one of the largest displays of oil lamps in the world; more than a million diyas dot the temple- and garden-lined waterfront come festival time. Lamp displays and laser and light shows also cement Ayodhya as a top spot for Diwali travelers. (Ayodhya is located 84 miles [135 km] from the state's capital, Lucknow.)

Cuisine is a staple of Diwali, and according to Rathod, who grew up in western India, each state has its own specialty, which you can sample on a tour. Some countrywide bites include *gulab jamun* (fried dough balls), *jalebi* (crisp and sweet spiral snacks), and *shankarpali* (flaky cookies served both sweet and salty).

WHERE TO STAY

To authentically embrace the Diwali holiday, ditch the hotel and book a homestay with a local family. This overnight option provides a deeper immersion into Indian culture, while simultaneously supporting local communities and businesses. Sites like Homestays of India list reputable options throughout the country.

TWILIGHT TIGER PATROL

Hike by night with a Periyar Tiger Reserve ranger.

BUDGET: $ **WHEN TO GO:** October–February   **ACTIVITY LEVEL:** Strenuous   **GO FOR:** Wildlife

What's that sound? On a night patrol through the Periyar Tiger Reserve in the mountains of southern India, it could be just about anything: elephants, wild pigs, leopards, macaques, or, if you're exceptionally lucky, a tiger—the elusive jungle cat this reserve was designed to protect.

Periyar is one of the oldest reserves in India, established in 1978. Its nighttime patrol tours, known as the Jungle Scout program, take visitors out into the evergreen woodlands with armed forest guards. Their weapons are not meant to protect you; these guards have been trained to defend the local wildlife against poaching.

The Periyar patrollers are from the local community and are part of an important project that extends beyond bucket-list tiger sightings. Indigenous and local communities, including former poachers, lead efforts—including the twilight patrols—to protect and conserve this biodiverse 300-square-mile (777 km²) forest. In turn, they reap the economic rewards of tiger tourism. (Research shows that wildlife tourism can be up to five times more lucrative than poaching.)

A night scout requires a degree of fitness. You'll trudge through the jungle by foot, listening for sounds and watching for even the faintest movements. The three-hour adventure runs overnight, and weaves through the buffer zone between the park and the local communities.

OPPOSITE: Look for tigers on a twilight tour in southern India's Periyar Tiger Reserve.

NEPAL

EVEREST BASE CAMP

Camp with fellow mountaineers on the world's highest peak.

BUDGET: $$$$$ **WHEN TO GO:** March–May or September–December
ACTIVITY LEVEL: Strenuous **GO FOR:** Adventure

Imagine dozing to the creak of shifting ice and waking to an amphitheater of sun-dappled Himalaya. This bucket-list night at Everest Base Camp could be yours—if you're willing to work for it.

From March to May and September to December, intrepid travelers can book an Everest Base Camp expedition that includes one or two nights at the legendary high-altitude campsite. The trek through Nepal's Sagarmatha National Park, which climbs toward the world-famous 29,032-foot (8,849 m) summit, will have you sharing air with some of the world's greatest climbers. Except, while these mountaineers are readying for a death-defying ascent to the top of the world, you'll be stopping at Base Camp, one of the last elevation points on Everest where human life is easily sustainable.

The human body operates best at sea level, with sufficient oxygen to support essential organs like the brain and lungs. The amount of oxygen available reduces as you climb, and these trimmed rates strain your body. You can begin to feel the effects of altitude, such as a headache or nausea, as low as 6,500 feet (2,000 m). The higher you go, the tougher it gets.

Everest Base Camp sits at around 17,500 feet (5,335 m), where climbers have about half the amount of available oxygen as they would at sea level with each breath. At the altitude just beyond Base Camp, the human body begins to decay. That's why many mountaineers follow a "climb high, sleep

OTHER MARVELS

There's another way to sleep at Everest Base Camp, but it'll require endurance. The Everest Marathon takes place over three weeks and includes trekking, acclimatization, Base Camp sleeps, and the grand finale: running 26.2 miles (42.2 km) from Base Camp across the Khumbu Valley's ice and snow via Sherpa trails.

OPPOSITE: The feat of dreams for many mountaineers, Everest's peak stands at 29,032 feet (8,849 m) above sea level.

PAGES 100-101: As many as 30,000 people reach Everest Base Camp every year.

low" acclimatization process, where they progress beyond Base Camp during the day, then sleep at the lower altitude until their bodies are ready for the next stage.

Base Camp tourist treks require around three weeks, and largely follow a similar itinerary up the mountain, with porters toting your gear and preparing camp. Trips include stints at Namche Bazaar, Everest's first acclimatization stop and the heartbeat of the Sherpa culture.

While you're there, visit Namche Bazaar's Sherpa museum and local market to embrace and honor the local community before trekking their sacred landscapes. From there, you'll continue skyward to the village of Dingboche, then Gorak Shep. Most Everest Base Camp treks head to the iconic tent-speckled camp for only a day visit, then return to Gorak Shep for the night.

A select few tour outfitters have permits for Base Camp overnights, including Highland Expeditions, Himalayan Glacier, and Ian Taylor Trekking. This option lets you camp alongside expeditioners, or even watch them tackle passes

TRAVEL TIP

The Sherpas, a Nepalese ethnic group native to the Himalaya, know these mountains intimately. Yet Sherpa climbing staff have long faced mistreatment, abuse, and even death. To support the local community with your trek, inquire about your outfitter's fair pay and porter safety policies—each porter should carry no more than 55 pounds (25 kg)—and prepare to tip fairly.

like Khumbu Icefall, one of the world's most dangerous ice climbing sites.

Evenings at Everest Base Camp are especially intoxicating, from dinner spent with professional climbers and Sherpa teams to the polka-dotted nightscape that awaits outside the mess tent door. While thousands of stars and the sparkly Milky Way delight every clear night of the trek, up here, at Earth's most sought-after campground, life feels like an IMAX film.

The Base Camp trek requires major advanced physical preparation. You'll face at least 12 grueling days of steep and high-altitude hiking, with a minimum of five hours of slogging each day.

Before climbing, plot your Leave No Trace plan. Mount Everest, particularly its camps, has struggled with littering and degradation in the past few decades. Be prepared to pack out all that you bring in, and rely on reusable supplies, such as water bottles.

ABOVE: Tibetans believe when the wind blows prayer flags, which line Everest Base Camp, it is spreading blessings and goodwill.

OPPOSITE: Climbers take on the challenge of Everest's steep and extreme terrain.

HOT-AIR BALLOON GLOW SHOW

Witness a desert festival full of color and sparkle.

BUDGET: $ **WHEN TO GO:** April–May **ACTIVITY LEVEL:** Mild **GO FOR:** Culture

Spring brings pageantry to Saudi Arabia's ancient AlUla desert, from a sea of harmonic hot-air balloons synchronously flashing to late-night astronomy sessions with all eyes on the star-splattered sky. The impetus for the country's spellbinding entertainment: the three-week AlUla Skies Festival, an annual celebration of the nightscapes that helped travelers and traders navigate this region for millennia.

Few experiences are as synonymous with the festival as its after-dark glow show, when anchored hot-air balloons illuminate to the beat of the blaring music. Over the years, Saudi Arabia has made a name for itself in the world of balloon displays with this magical event. In 2022, it set the Guinness World Record for the planet's largest hot-air balloon glow show with 142 of the shimmering vessels bobbing at once.

You can catch the rainbow-hued entertainment during weekend nights at the free-admission Skies Festival, which runs from late April into May. The glow show is held in Hegra's Winter Park; the synchronized performance lasts roughly an hour.

For another awe-striking view, board a balloon before sunrise for an aerial glimpse of Hegra, Saudi Arabia's first UNESCO World Heritage site. This sliver of desert, with its winding streets and colossal tombs carved from boulders, was a prime stop on the ancient incense trading route.

OPPOSITE: **About 150 hot-air balloons take to the sky during the three-week AlUla Skies Festival.**

JORDAN

PETRA BY CANDLELIGHT

Navigate ancient sandstone passageways beneath the stars.

BUDGET: **$**   WHEN TO GO: **Year-round**   ACTIVITY LEVEL: **Intermediate**   GO FOR: **Culture**

A jaunt through southwest Jordan's labyrinth of canyons and camel-dotted corridors leads to one of the world's most mysterious and enthralling ancient cities: Petra. By day, the sandstone escape, once an ancient capital, draws hundreds of thousands of travelers with its millennia-old backstory. But come at dusk to see the marvel in a new, candlelit light.

The twilight experience, Petra by Night, provides a sensory immersion into the city's storied history, with mint tea and soft woodwind melodies to help set the scene.

Petra's journey from ancient capital to UNESCO World Heritage site to one of the New Seven Wonders of the World is about as winding as its canyons. Squished between the Red and Dead Seas, the desert wonder was a core stopover on the region's ancient trading routes. The Nabataeans, a group of Arabian nomads, knew the area well, and a steady stream of ivory, textile, and spice traders paid them good money for their savvy desert shelters and intel.

Over time, the Nabataeans acquired enough riches to create their own capital—present-day Petra. The once nomadic people carved houses, tombs, and palaces by hand into the copper sandstone. They decked these structures in traditional stucco and maneuvered intricate underground funnels to make water readily available in an otherwise arid destination.

OPPOSITE: Candlelight paper lanterns guide visitors to the sandstone wonders of Petra.

PAGES 108-109: Visitors sit before the intricately carved Treasury, which glows by candlelight.

Around A.D. 106, the Roman Empire swooped in and took control of the Nabataean hub. By A.D. 363, a powerful earthquake had destroyed much of it, including its lifeblood: the Nabataean water system. Many capital dwellers fled. Centuries later, western explorers rediscovered Petra, and soon after it became an archaeological attraction. Tourism spiked.

Today, Petra is one of Jordan's top tourist attractions. It's open to the public daily, with Petra by Night running three times a week between 8:30 and 10:30 p.m. If time allows, visit during daytime as well. Day and night tours complement each other, with deep history and sightseeing by day and spellbinding scenery once the sun sets.

The latter, a more tranquil experience, lets you see Petra like the Nabataeans. More than 1,500 candles dot the 30-minute amble from the Siq gorge to the glowing Treasury—the famous facade once used as a tomb for royals. Take a seat on a woven blanket to admire the view and let the echoing Bedouin music lead you back in time.

OTHER MARVELS

For millennia, traders traversed Jordan's basalt and sandstone deserts toting spices and incense. Now, you can trek in their footsteps on the Jordan Trail, nicknamed the Inca Trail of the Middle East. The 400-mile (640 km) route links more than 50 villages from north to south Jordan, including a stretch near Petra. You can hike the route in sections, but you'll need at least a month and a half to complete the full trip.

WADI RUM GLAMPING

Feel like you've spent a night on Mars in this otherworldly desert.

BUDGET: $$ **WHEN TO GO:** July–September   **ACTIVITY LEVEL:** Intermediate   **GO FOR:** Stargazing

Wadi Rum has often been compared to Mars—and, in fact, it has been used to represent the planet in numerous TV and movie productions. Striated djebels tower above rust-tinged sand fields, with red rocks stretching to the horizon. As darkness descends, the Technicolor Milky Way streaks across the sky, making the entire setting feel otherworldly. You can escape to this Martian landscape—and sleep on it—with a night of Wadi Rum glamping.

This 280-square-mile (725 km²) swath of red sand is nearly the size of New York City and sits one mile (1.6 km) above sea level. It's a dry, arid climate with virtually no light pollution. That makes for near-perfect stargazing conditions, an added perk for the abundance of glamping sites that have turned Wadi Rum into an astrotourism gem.

Of course, glampers were hardly the first to recognize the ancient desert's light-freckled night skies. The Bedouin people used the mountains and constellations to navigate the scorched valley. The terrain has been a staple on migration routes since the Stone Age. In fact, historians believe humans have lived in the Wadi Rum desert for at least 12,000 years based on the abundance of ancient rock drawings and petroglyphs.

Few Bedouin people remain nomadic today, but many have opened culture-meets-adventure tourism offerings in the region to help travelers

WHILE YOU'RE THERE

Wadi Rum is one of the world's most lauded desert rock climbing destinations. Bedouin people have been ascending these routes for millennia to hunt ibex, and you can try it for yourself with locally run outfitters like Shabab Sahra.

OPPOSITE: Glass yurts at the Memories Aicha Luxury Camp in Wadi Rum offer cozy digs with views of the desert skies.

PAGES 112-113: At Bedouin camps, like Wadi Rum Starlight Camp, follow a daytime camel ride tour through the valley with evening stargazing.

see the desert, its history, and the stars through their ancestors' eyes.

For the most authentic trip, book lodging at a Bedouin-owned camp. These getaways include traditional goat-hair tents and campfire-cooked meals, as well as guided stargazing experiences from local experts. Wadi Rum Starlight Camp, a Bedouin overnight spot with mountain-view tents and jeep, camel, or hiking tours available by day, provides open valley views for unparalleled nightscapes from your bed or tent door.

For a night of constellation-gazing from your sleeping bag, consider open-air camping, also known as bivouac camping. Local outfitter Bedouin Campsite and Tours runs alfresco sleep excursions in shallow desert caves, known as *tors,* which Bedouin nomads long used for shelter from the rain.

Wadi Rum, proclaimed a UNESCO World Heritage site in 2011, may look devoid of animal life by day, but at night critters such gerbils, lizards, and up to eight scorpion species may appear. Keep an eye out and listen for the faint sounds of scurrying or rustling.

Most Wadi Rum trips start in Rum Village, the desert's tourism entrance gate. It's located around two hours from Petra (page 106). Though you technically can visit the desert year-round, guides say summer, particularly around a new moon, is the best time for stargazing.

FLUORESCENT DIVING

See the ocean take on new life after dark.

BUDGET: $$ **WHEN TO GO:** Year-round   **ACTIVITY LEVEL:** Intermediate   **GO FOR:** Wildlife

Joining a fluorescent night dive is like swimming through the set of a sci-fi film. Cherry-hued seahorses sway with the currents. Acid green coral tentacles squiggle along the seafloor. In your periphery, glow-in-the-dark fish, sharks, and sea turtles glide elegantly through the water.

"It's almost as though you're entering a different dimension," says Ahmed Mujthaba, owner of Maldives-based Mujavaz Scuba and Travels. "Everything around you is fluorescing." Mujthaba leads fluorescent night dive tours throughout the Maldives, where the tropical waters have an abundance of after-dark radiance.

This underwater outing lets you in on one of the animal kingdom's most perplexing puzzles: a secret illuminated language we're only beginning to understand. Humans view the world differently than most wildlife, particularly when it comes to color. Many creatures' eyes pick up light wavelengths we can't see, such as ultraviolet. When UV light shines on these animals, their bodies absorb the light and reemit it in a different wavelength, which appears as a different color. This is not to be confused with bioluminescence, where animals create their own light.

Biofluorescence is common among terrestrial animals like the platypus and southern flying squirrel. It's also rampant throughout the ocean. More

WHERE TO STAY

Climate change and human impact put Maldives reefs at risk. Resorts like Soneva Fushi, located in the Baa Atoll UNESCO Biosphere Reserve, give travelers a lower-impact way to enjoy the pristine islands. Half the resort's electricity runs on renewable energy. It's also 90 percent waste free.

OPPOSITE: A diver's flashlight illuminates a school of pennant bannerfish.

PAGES 116-117: From shore, you can spot bioluminescent creatures in the shallow waters of the Maldives.

than 200 fish are known to use biofluorescence, as are certain sharks, eels, corals, seahorses, and sea turtles.

Some scientists believe animals use biofluorescence as color-coded language for interspecies communication; others think it's for finding prey, hiding from predators, or attracting mates. Research shows biofluorescence is especially prevalent among small fish that appear well camouflaged to the human eye, such as the lizard fish. These species, nicknamed cryptic fish, are up to 70 times more likely to glow than their more visible peers.

A fluorescent night dive is one of the easiest ways to eavesdrop on these peculiar neon conversations. To see it, divers use a blue light and yellow mask filters—a combination that lets you see the ocean through the eyes of a fish. "Anemones and entire coral heads will light up in vivid blues and greens," says Mujthaba. "I'd compare it to watching fireworks. The intensity of the colors is spectacular against a dark night backdrop of the ocean water."

CRITTER CORNER

The Maldives' glowing fish and corals may put on a surreal show, but they're not the animal kingdom's only after-dark entertainment. Indian flying foxes, among the world's largest fruit-eating bats, soar from island to island, spreading seeds that support local ecosystems along the way. Watch for these herbivores around dusk; they're found on most Maldivian islands, and with a wingspan of up to five feet (1.5 m), they're hard to miss.

You can float through this intergalactic disco via dive spots all over the world, from Bonaire in the Dutch Caribbean to the Atlantic coast of Florida. The biodiverse Indo-Pacific region is especially known for bright displays, including island nations like the Maldives, where Mujthaba says the South Male and Ari Atolls promise the most scenic fluorescent excursions.

These atolls teem with reef fish and corals. Most dive sites are also far from city lights, which enhances the neon hues. To further amplify the colors, set out during a new moon.

To partake in a fluorescent dive, you'll need at least an open water diving certification from the Professional Association of Diving Instructors (PADI). Given the blue lights are fainter than most after-dark dive torches, a specific night dive certification is a bonus. And, though it's less common, some guides, such as Mujthaba, lead fluorescent night snorkels for nondiving travelers too.

PART THREE

EUROPE

The illuminated Eiffel Tower (page 174) stands above other glowing icons of Paris, including the Champs-Élysées (at left).

CHRISTMAS MARKETS

Unleash the holiday spirit with lights, bites, and cheer.

BUDGET: $ **WHEN TO GO:** November–January   **ACTIVITY LEVEL:** Mild   **GO FOR:** Culture

With twinkling lights and the aroma of fresh-baked sweets filling the air, European Christmas markets could turn even the grumpiest Scrooge into a merrymaker. Thousands of these festive gathering spots fill cities across the continent. Some transform small towns into real-life snow globes. Others give bustling big city dwellers permission to slow down and savor the season.

Records of the earliest known European Christmas market, Vienna's Dezembermarkt (December market), date back to the late 1200s—though it didn't always have today's jovial holiday vibe. Back then, merchants brought their goods to one central December market to help residents stock up to survive the grueling winter. Decades later, the cheery holiday market tradition took shape in Germany, particularly Dresden.

These days, it's hard to find a European country that doesn't celebrate the season with decked-out hangouts. Though you can visit during the day, the markets really come to life after dusk, when the decorations sparkle, sound and light shows come to life, and mulled wine is sipped well past dark.

Germany alone has more than 2,500 Christmas markets. Don't miss Dresden's Striezelmarkt, one of the country's oldest. Dresden, the capital of Saxony, wows with the world's largest Weihnachtspyramide, a multilevel wooden pyramid first created by woodworkers in the nearby Erzgebirge mountain region.

BEST BITES

Glühwein, a hot mulled wine with notes of citrus, cinnamon, cloves, and star anise, has been a staple in the European holiday market scene for centuries, but it actually dates back to the second-century Roman Empire. Romans used the wine to stay warm and healthy during winter.

OPPOSITE: More than 70 stalls offer mulled wine, roasted almonds, and wooden art at the Christmas market in Annaberg-Buchholz, Germany.

PAGES 124-125: Christmas decorations are displayed for sale at Nuremberg's Christkindlesmarkt.

Striezelmarkt's 48-foot-tall (15 m) tower rises above the buzzing main square; festive figurines and candles decorate each tier, and a spinning windmill and star grace the top. Grab mulled wine and traditional *pflaumentoffel* (an edible chimney-sweep figurine made of dried plums) from the A-frame stalls, then head for the sky-high Ferris wheel for a bird's-eye view of the bustling incandescent main square.

In France, Strasbourg's Christmas markets have been a city staple since 1570. More than 300 festival stalls line these half-timber streets, with whiffs of spiced wine, roasted nuts, and baked bites all competing for air space. The star of the show is the city's nearly 100-foot-tall (30 m) Christmas tree—one of Europe's tallest decorated natural trees. The soaring pine draws travelers to Place Kléber, where fairy light–swathed stalls dish out steamy *vin chaud* (mulled wine) and hot cocoa as ice skaters glide beside bedecked Aubette palace, an 18th-century landmark.

Brussels, Belgium's fairy tale–like capital city, brims with holiday fervor during its annual

TRAVEL TIP

So many markets, so little time. Make the most of your winter trip to Europe with a Christmas market river cruise. Adventures by Disney runs weeklong Rhine River floats with stops at holiday hangouts in Switzerland, France, Germany, and the Netherlands. Or board an eight-day Danube River jaunt to soak up the festive lights and bites in Germany, Austria, and Hungary.

Christmas market, a five-week event that transforms its baroque and Gothic Grand-Place into a scene straight from the North Pole. Brussels' festivities are a mosaic of merriment: a fantastical 360-degree sound and light show projected on the historic buildings, a 180-foot-tall (55 m) Ferris wheel that overlooks the city's winter wonderland, and more than a mile (1.6 km) of glittery chalet stalls to stock up on handmade gifts, warm drinks, and fresh waffles.

In Budapest, Vörösmarty, the city's longest-running Christmas market, draws crowds with enchanting lights and traditional Hungarian delights. Evening bathes the Gründerzeit-style Café Gerbeaud, a century-old coffeehouse, in rich color with an hourly sound and light show. And aromatic treats like *kürtőskalács* (a cinnamon pastry known as chimney cake) and *dödölles* (potato dumplings) make the Vörösmarty market a multisensory affair.

ETHNOCOSMOLOGY MUSEUM

Discover our connection to the universe at this Baltic museum.

BUDGET: $ **WHEN TO GO:** Year-round   **ACTIVITY LEVEL:** Mild   **GO FOR:** Stargazing

ithuania's Ethnocosmology Museum looks like a portal to space—and, in a way, it is. The architectural marvel, a set of silver towers with a panoramic orb piercing above the surrounding pines, is a first-of-its-kind museum dedicated to ethnocosmology, a field that studies humankind's relationship with the sun, moon, and night sky.

You'll find this cosmic venue near Lake Želvos in northeast Lithuania's quaint, forested village of Kulionys, around 40 miles (65 km) from the capital city, Vilnius. Half the museum is dedicated to ethnocosmology; the other half runs night sky tours of deep space objects led by local astronomers.

This countryside complex is an adequate distance from any major city to allow for remote, dark skies with minimal light pollution. Space observations take place with both the naked eye, and 40- and 80-millimeter telescopes. Another 10 minutes down the road is Molėtai Astronomical Observatory, where you can look through more high-powered telescopes.

Guided tours highlight artifacts, such as texts and songs dedicated to the sky. An exterior exhibition with an oversize model of the solar system and a spatial sundial builds upon the curriculum, illustrating how early humans relied on interstellar objects for timekeeping and agriculture.

The museum is open year-round: If you're visiting in summer, be prepared to stay up late; the sun doesn't set until around 10 p.m.

OPPOSITE: Lithuania's futuristic Ethnocosmology Museum houses an underground gallery and observation tower with a powerful telescope. There's also an exhibition space outside.

ICELAND

HOT SPRING AURORA HUNTING

Marvel at two of Iceland's natural wonders in one dreamy night.

BUDGET: $–$$$ **WHEN TO GO:** September–April   **ACTIVITY LEVEL:** Mild   **GO FOR:** Aurora chasing

A successful aurora hunt doesn't require chattering teeth on a snowbank or glacier. In parts of Iceland, you can chase the northern lights in nothing but a swimsuit. Your perch? A steamy hot spring. Naturally heated pools attract soakers throughout the Land of Fire and Ice, and most swimmable sites hover around 100°F (37.7°C). The result: a tranquil night with two of Iceland's beloved natural wonders—geothermal energy and the aurora borealis.

Iceland has geography to thank for the first wonder, geothermal energy. The country straddles the Mid-Atlantic Ridge, one of the planet's most significant fault lines where the North American and Eurasian tectonic plates drift apart at a rate of around 0.8 inches (2 cm) each year. Diverging plates have created an upswelling of heated rock from Earth's mantle, known as a plume. Scientists believe the plume, which lies just 12 miles (19 km) beneath Iceland's surface, originates in Earth's sweltering mantle, where temperatures are at minimum 1832°F (1000°C). Water on Iceland's surface seeps into the toasty bedrock, is heated by the magma, then trickles back up. This creates Iceland's bounty of more than 700 known geothermic spots.

Auroras are another renowned Iceland draw. Kaleidoscopic northern lights, sparked when charged particles from the sun collide with our atmosphere, congregate in doughnut-shaped zones above Earth's magnetic

FAST FACT

In Iceland, geothermal energy offers more than a tranquil dip. It powers roughly 90 percent of the country's heating and 30 percent of its electricity. It also warms the streets to melt snow and keeps greenhouses toasty for fresh produce year-round.

OPPOSITE: Enjoy a view of the northern lights from a natural hot spring in Iceland's Westfjords.

PAGES 132-133: Watch the aurora borealis from the warmth of a hot tub at luxury resorts near Kirkjufell (Church Mountain) in western Iceland.

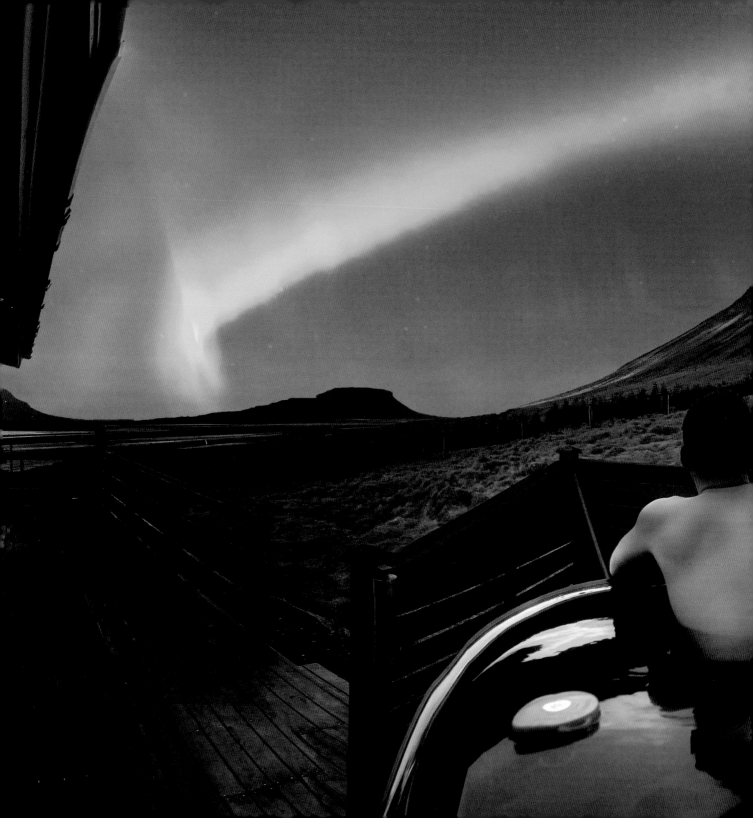

poles, around 65 to 70 degrees north and south of the Equator. With Iceland's location between 63 and 66 degrees north, it's in the heart of the auroral action. Many travelers head to the country solely to spot the night show. During the northern lights season, September through April, the sky dances with brilliant streaks on more than 100 nights, pending cloud cover.

You're within driving distance of a solid soak from just about anywhere in the country. Booking a hotel with an on-site hot pool is the most convenient and safest way to have a heated dip beneath auroras. For that, your options abound.

In Selfoss, a small town on Iceland's Golden Circle route, Ion Adventure Hotel greets guests with mossy lava fields, snow-flecked mountains, and an outdoor soaking pool that overlooks both. The nearby Mount Hengill volcano is technically active, though it's not expected to erupt for thousands of years. Instead, it produces heat for the region, including the hotel and its cozy pool. Watch for the lights during an evening swim, and don't miss the property's Northern Lights Bar,

OTHER MARVELS

Don't just dip in Iceland's toasty hot springs; see the sizzling substance that warms them. The Lava Show in southern Iceland—one of the world's only live lava exhibitions—is an experiential and narrated demonstration dedicated to the bright orange goo. Over the course of the 50-minute show, you'll learn about Icelandic volcanism, then don safety glasses as real lava oozes and bubbles before your eyes.

ABOVE: The Blue Lagoon is Iceland's most famous geothermal spa. Its mineral water is known for its skin-healing properties.

OPPOSITE: Northern lights sightings are frequent above Kirkjufell (Church Mountain).

where floor-to-ceiling windows let you chase auroras with the hotel's signature Sweet Black Death—a Brennivín and blueberry liqueur cocktail—in hand.

For a farther-flung dip beneath the northern lights, head five hours north of Reykjavík to the country's craggy Westfjords. This rural northwestern peninsula is about as rugged as Iceland gets, with dizzying cliffside drives and snowy flat-topped mountains. Heydalur, a guesthouse on a working horse farm, offers multiple on-site hot pools that stay open all night. Don't be surprised if a shaggy white pony joins your aurora borealis gazing.

You can also chase the lights in one of Iceland's many late-night public pools. Try Myvatn Nature Baths, a collection of milky blue soak spots in Iceland's mountainous north. Geosea, in the fishing town of Húsavík, overlooks Skjálfandi Bay, where mountains meet the ocean. Come summer, your evening dip will coincide with another phenomenon: 24 hours of daylight.

LAS FALLAS

Watch the fiery conclusion to an iconic celebration.

BUDGET: $ **WHEN TO GO: March**   **ACTIVITY LEVEL: Mild**   **GO FOR: Culture**

Puffs of smoke, the streets ablaze—these are the telltale signs that Valencia's Noche de la Cremà has commenced. This annual spring event marks the end of the city's cherished Las Fallas festival, a centuries-old happening that blends art, humor, and friendly competition to kick off the new season. And what better way to welcome the warmer months than sending hundreds of intricate sculptures up in flames?

March's Las Fallas, inscribed to UNESCO's Representative List of the Intangible Cultural Heritage of Humanity in 2016, is an ode to St. Joseph, the patron saint of carpenters. Centuries ago, Valencian carpenters erected lights on wooden beams to safely work through the dark winter. They bid adieu to winter's frosty days by burning the beams each spring. The earliest written record of this tradition dates back to the 18th century.

Today's Las Fallas is a twist on those woodworking infernos. Neighborhoods across Valencia create their own *falla*, a monument made of intricate and lifelike statues and dolls, known as *ninots*. The fallas are like dioramas; each depicts culturally relevant scenes, often as political satire. They're constructed via a host of materials: cardboard, wood, papier-mâché, and plaster. The goal is to outdo other neighborhoods and festival participants, not just in size—although some figurines reach up to 100 feet (30 m) tall—but also in creativity. One year brought Yoda and Chewbacca, another an ode to Mick Jagger.

The full celebration runs from March 1 to 19, with the bulk of festivities during the final four days. During the latter stretch, you can admire hundreds of these statues throughout the city. Officials close roads so pedestrians can admire the

OPPOSITE: Neighbors compete to create the most intricate *fallas*, many of which feature well-known characters or demonstrate political satire.

PAGES 138-139: All but the year's winning *fallas* are set ablaze during the festival.

fallas, with street vendors serving up local bites, like *bunyols de carabassa* (pumpkin fritters), as part of the festivities.

The sculptures remain on display until the much anticipated final night: March 19, better known as Noche de la Cremà, which coincides with St. Joseph's Day. At this twilight bonanza, the ninots are engulfed in flames. A popular vote, which runs from February to mid-March, spares one lucky ninot from the burn each year. The chosen sculpture is displayed in Valencia's year-round Fallas Museum alongside decades worth of its fellow pardonees.

You can admire the monuments and their burns all over town. The monuments adorn most street corners and main squares. Expect crowds around the winning fallas, announced in the first week of the festival via Visit Valencia. You can go on your own or book a local guide, such as Tours in Valencia, for history of the festival and help navigating the best burns. Don't forget your party pants; once the fires commence, charismatic sing-along songs and traditional dancing fill the streets.

WHILE YOU'RE THERE

Valencia's futuristic City of Arts and Sciences is aptly named; the nearly 3.7-million-square-foot (344,000 m²) complex is like its own village, with areas centered on everything from oceanography to performance arts. Don't miss the experiential science museum, particularly the third floor, which is dedicated to the history of the universe, from big bang to present.

MEET KRAMPUS

Spend the night with Austria's frightening holiday figure.

BUDGET: $ **WHEN TO GO:** December   **ACTIVITY LEVEL:** Mild   **GO FOR:** Culture

Keep your eyes open if you find yourself in Austria in early December. A frightening Krampus—or hundreds of them—could appear at any turn. This beast of a creature, with its scaly horns, oversize tongue, and threatening claws, is synonymous with the holiday season in the alpine region of Bavaria. Although St. Nicholas delights children with presents and cheer on December 6, creepy Krampus, the half-goat, half-demon celebrated on December 5, reminds little ones to behave. Those who don't could get lugged away in Krampus's oversize bag.

Though Krampus is celebrated around Christmastime, the whip-cracking monster got its start in pagan roots. Many link Krampus to the son of Hel, the underworld's Norse god. Today, December 5 marks Krampusnacht (Krampus Night), when children leave shoes outside their bedrooms and await either a treat for being good, or a rod that means they're naughty. Either on or during the weekend leading up to the holiday, parades of costumed partygoers fill the streets. These events, known as Krampus runs, flood the roads and alleyways with dozens, and sometimes hundreds, of Krampuses dinging bells, wearing grizzly masks, and making merry mischief.

The Krampus frenzies can occur at any hour of the day, but many, particularly the wildest ones, hit at night. The chilling costumes are actually quite elaborate. The garb can take months to create, many with real horns and fur, and some are passed down through generations.

Learn about the beast's past and present via the Krampus Museum in Kitzbühel, around 50 miles (80 km) southwest of Salzburg.

OPPOSITE: The horned figure of Krampus reminds kids to be on their best behavior.

DOGSLED UNDER AN AURORA

Experience a night of mushing and cosmic magic.

BUDGET: $$–$$$ **WHEN TO GO:** November–January   **ACTIVITY LEVEL:** Intermediate   **GO FOR:** Aurora chasing

I f chasing the aurora borealis tops your bucket list, we have one better: hunting those cosmic swirls from the seat of an Arctic dogsled. Add to the mix the backdrop of ice-laden Svalbard, a Norwegian archipelago 650 miles (1,050 km) from the North Pole, and you're in for the aurora chase of your life.

Svalbard lies well above the Arctic Circle; its capital, Longyearbyen, is the world's northernmost permanently inhabited town. Given its extreme-north setting, the island hosts some of the most extensive northern lights and space-weather research facilities. You can spot lime and lavender scribbles across the sky here from late September through mid-March. Mid-November to January, when the region plummets into more than two months without sunlight, is particularly special. That around-the-clock darkness means you could even catch the lights over lunch.

To admire the snow-frosted tundra and pursue the polar sky show, join an after-dark dogsledding tour. The transportation method has long been integral to Arctic culture, with archaeological evidence dating it to around A.D. 1000. Researchers believe Inuit communities in present-day northern Canada were the first to hone it. Dogsledding eventually spread across the polar regions and was even used during World War I.

A millennium's worth of technological advancements, such as snowmobiles, have reshaped transit in the Arctic. Even so, many communities,

OPPOSITE: On your dogsledding tour, the pack will occasionally stop so you can photograph—or just stare in awe at—the beauty of the aurora borealis.

PAGES 144-145: The aurora borealis dances above Norway's Lofoten archipelago, known for its small villages, dramatic peaks, and frequent sightings of the northern lights.

including Longyearbyen, still keep the tradition alive, largely through tourism engagement.

For a northern lights jaunt, you'll hit the sled at nightfall. The fun begins with a sled dog meet and greet before taking off into the white abyss. Each guest gets to play musher (driver) for part of the journey. When you're not leading the pack, you'll be tucked under a blanket in the sled's seat. Keep your eyes on the sky. One quick pulse of light could signal other neon ribbons to follow.

The trip concludes with more quality pup time back at home base. Alternatively, take your dog-sled aurora chase farther with an overnight trip; it's like hut-to-hut backpacking, but in this case, the pups are the ones doing the work.

Fun is guaranteed on these Arctic adventures, but northern lights sightings are not. You need clear, dark skies with minimal clouds and an active aurora to catch the show. Be prepared for frigid conditions: Gloves, thick coats, snow boots, hats, and hand warmers are musts. If the snow hasn't hit by your visit, fear not—Svalbard mushers have evolved to offer dogsleds with wheels.

FAST FACT

Aurora research is just one of Svalbard's important contributions to the world. The bedrock above Svalbard's Longyearbyen airport also holds the key to the world's food supply: the Global Seed Vault. This protective hub, nicknamed the "doomsday vault," stores more than 930,000 varieties of crops as an insurance policy on Earth's food reserves.

ITALY

THE COLOSSEUM AFTER DARK

Tour Rome's most famous ruin by moonlight.

BUDGET: $ **WHEN TO GO:** Year-round   **ACTIVITY LEVEL:** Mild   **GO FOR:** Culture

The warm-glowing Colosseum is a highlight of Rome's nightscapes, but you don't have to admire the marvel from afar. After-dark trips to the famous amphitheater are available via guided tour and offer an enchanting and less crowded way to enjoy one of Italy's most famed attractions.

These twilight outings explore lesser seen sides of the Colosseum, such as the hypogeum. Gladiators and animals, including bears, wolves, and leopards, were held in these dark underground tunnels before being let loose to fight. On a night tour, you can stride in the gladiators' footsteps from the hypogeum to the arena entrance gate, then step onto the arena floor as moonlight bathes the 50,000-some seats towering above you.

This immersive excursion shows the real side of the millennia-old Colosseum, which has a somber history. Thousands of people—and even more animals—lost their lives across the four centuries that the Colosseum was in use. Guided visits, booked through outfitters like Discover Rome Tours, include narration about the past and present of this architectural marvel. Many night trips also feature a stop at the adjacent Roman Forum, once a bustling gathering place for the ancient empire, that's particularly enchanting after dark.

Though nighttime Colosseum outings run intermittently year-round, they're most available from summer through fall. Book early; tours often sell out.

OPPOSITE: Get an after-hours—and less crowded—view of the Colosseum with a guided night tour of the amphitheater.

TWILIGHT TRUFFLE HUNTS

Forage for treasured fungi after the sun goes down.

BUDGET: $$$ **WHEN TO GO:** November–December   **ACTIVITY LEVEL:** Intermediate   **GO FOR:** Culture

I t only takes one bite to fall in love with Italy's decadent white truffles, some of the rarest and most expensive truffles on the planet. In Piedmont, you can take your enthusiasm for the rich, earthy fungus up a notch with an after-dark truffle hunt—foraging dogs very much included.

Truffles have been part of Italy's culture for millennia, if not longer. "There are records of truffle hunting from ancient Romans to Greeks," says Enad Germani of the Italian Truffle Hunting Association, AssoTartufai. In Germani's family alone, foraging knowledge spans five generations. Italy's deep truffle roots helped the foraging tradition nab a spot on the UNESCO Representative List of the Intangible Cultural Heritage of Humanity in 2021.

The country's white truffle, in particular, is a crowd-pleaser. It's the most fragrant of all truffles, with a powerful musky aroma and soft, almost garlicky, taste. Chefs often shave it raw atop dishes like pasta and eggs.

The mouthwatering ingredient grows just beneath the forest floor via a symbiotic relationship with tree roots, most often oaks, beeches, hazels, and poplars. Woodland creatures such as boars, birds, and badgers unintentionally carry the truffle spores, helping the fungus disperse and thrive. You can find these treasures throughout Italy; in regions like Piedmont, near the Italian Alps, the coveted truffles are especially prolific. It's also

FAST FACT

The planet's most expensive edible fungus, the white truffle, can sell for up to $3,000 a kilogram. According to Guinness World Records, the most expensive fungus sold at auction to date—a single white truffle weighing 3.3 pounds (1.5 kg)—went for $330,000 in 2007.

OPPOSITE: **Truffle hunter Rino Patrone shows off the bounty of his and his dog's foraging efforts.**

PAGES 150-151: **Truffle-sniffing dogs help find the valuable fungi, which foragers carefully collect.**

one of the only places with tours to hunt for the fungi after dark, says Germani, who leads twilight truffle-foraging trips in the region. These after-hours searches have long been a staple for Piedmont truffle hunters, who farm by day and scour the forest at night. The timing is also strategic. Soil aeration makes the truffle scent stronger, and the dogs are more focused without daytime distractions.

On these fungi outings, you'll meander among trees in lockstep with the trip's lead truffle hunter and their trained dog, typically the curly, purebred Lagotto Romagnolo breed. The duo's teamwork is astounding. "We describe it as being a single animal, with six legs and a tail," says Germani.

The canine scours the forest floor for a whiff of the lauded white truffle. Sometimes they strike gold within minutes. Other times it can take hours. When the scent hits, the giddy dog kicks up dirt until their owner arrives with a hoe for careful investigation. At this point, precision is key. Any dent in the truffle could reduce its value. During your trip, you can learn to dig up the truffle yourself.

The moonlit excursion runs for a few hours, beginning around 8 p.m. If the pup hits the jackpot, you can buy the freshly foraged truffle before you depart. If not, head to the local market to secure your bounty the next day.

Late fall is the best time to find the white truffle, particularly from November to December.

UP HELLY AA FESTIVAL

Prepare for spring like a Viking—flames and all.

BUDGET: $ **WHEN TO GO:** January   **ACTIVITY LEVEL:** Mild   **GO FOR:** Culture

S wirling orange flames pierce the coal black sky as nearly 1,000 costumed revelers march through the port town of Lerwick in the Shetland Islands, a craggy Scottish archipelago between the Faroe Islands and Norway. Some silver-helmeted revelers carry axes, shields, and torches. Others lug a 32-foot-long (10 m) replica Viking longship on wheels.

The merriment, known as the Up Helly Aa festival, is part of an annual midwinter celebration that starts with a firecracker and ends with a bonfire burning the longboat that required some 1,200 hours to build.

Vikings settled this area during the eighth and ninth centuries and lived here as farmers for nearly 600 years before the Shetlands came under Scottish rule in the 15th century. Although Up Helly Aa parades and festivals weren't a Viking custom, the centuries-old tradition honors the archipelago's Nordic history. The festivities, however, do at least partially stem from the Norse celebration of the sun's return after winter solstice.

Since the late 1800s, the islands' capital Lerwick has claimed the largest Up Helly Aa event. On the last Tuesday of January, its fervor and flames fill the Lerwick streets with hundreds to thousands of decked-out marchers and even more spectators who revel in the dark, cold winter night with torches, fire, live music, and fun.

OTHER MARVELS

Fires aren't the only winter delight in Shetland. The island's high-latitude location—it's on the same latitude as Norway, and closer to the Arctic Circle than to London—makes it perfect for viewing the northern lights, known locally as the "mirrie dancers"; *mirr* **means "to shimmer."**

OPPOSITE: Dressed as Vikings, revelers parade past the bonfire of the Up Helly Aa festival.

PAGES 154-155: The festival includes a parade through the streets, with participants dressed in full armor and carrying flags.

After the community's months of hard work to get festival ready—from carving the replica boat to hand-sewing costumes—Up Helly Aa officially begins with a flare shot into the sky. Participants follow the year's festival leader, the Guizer Jarl, who dresses and acts as a Norse ruler. Guizer Jarl has a squad of about two dozen official *guizers*, all decked in steel helmets and fur tunics. Vikings in the Jarl Squad are joined on the parade route by nearly 900 unofficial costumed guizers. The congregation carries flame-topped torches while snaking through town to the beat of traditional brass-band melodies, such as the Up Helly Aa song, which pays tribute to the past and future of this important event.

The parade begins along Hillhead Street; from there, guizers tote the replica longboat through town for 30 minutes en route to an open field, where the bonfire begins. Upon reaching the field, the teams secure the boat, stand back, and sling their torches at the center

CRITTER CORNER

Shetland ponies have been a staple of the islands for millennia. Scientists believe they walked across ice fields from southern Europe to reach the region after the last ice age, and evolved into the hardy, thick-furred ponies seen about the islands today. You'll likely spot the short and stocky equines on your trip—owners let them freely graze along the moorland—but you can also interact with and learn about them via the family-owned Shetland Pony Experience, located 12 miles (19 km) from Lerwick.

ABOVE: It takes about 1,200 hours to build the replica Viking longboat that is subsequently set on fire during the centuries-old celebration.

OPPOSITE: Revelers carry torches, ready to set the Viking longboat ablaze.

of the ship until it bursts into flames—a symbol of sunny days on the horizon. The sea of marigold ignites even more celebrations, including an evening of dancing and comedy sketches in the town's halls and gathering spaces (advanced tickets required).

To view the Up Helly Aa parade, head to Hillhead for the torch lighting. Or find a perch on St. Olaf or Harbour Streets to watch the burn site from a safe distance. Though the Lerwick festival is the most attended and well known of these events, other Shetland Up Helly Aa nights are held on South Mainland—the second largest Up Helly Aa—and Brae. Both take place in March, when you'll also have more daylight hours to enjoy the archipelago.

If you can't visit during the main event, the Up Helly Aa Exhibition in the Galley Shed runs from May until September with memorabilia and photographs from previous years.

MOUNTAINTOP BONFIRES

Witness Austria's summer solstice in all its glow.

BUDGET: $–$$ **WHEN TO GO:** June **ACTIVITY LEVEL:** Mild **GO FOR:** Culture

A ustria's hills may be alive with the sound of music, but the summer solstice brings another reason to adore the country's stunning panoramas: nighttime bonfires. In late June, hills and mountaintops throughout the country shimmer with bright orange blazes. It's a timeless ode to the longest day of the year—one you can admire throughout the country, but particularly in the Tyrol region.

Austria's late June bonfires are a mix of pagan and Catholic traditions. Throughout the Middle Ages, many pagans used the blazes to ward off demons and evil spirits. In 1796, the people of Tyrol swore an oath to the Sacred Heart of Jesus to protect the region against the invading French troops. They lit fires atop the peaks to symbolize the oath and continue to do so as part of June's Feast of the Sacred Heart of Jesus.

Across the country, rugged slopes flicker as pyres in the shapes of hearts and crosses ignite. In recent years, the local masterminds behind the mountaintop bonfire motifs have gotten creative, with modern designs such as flowers, animals, and cartoon favorites like Papa Smurf and Donald Duck.

These fires aren't part of an organized countrywide initiative. Instead, local organizations and communities host them. The teams spend months mapping out the images and ordering supplies. Then in June, either on summer solstice or the weeks surrounding it, the groups schlep their gear to their

WHERE TO STAY

Snooze 5,849 feet (1,783 m) above Austria's Salzkammergut lake district at Hotel Schafbergspitze. The lodge lies on the summit of Schafberg mountain. Hotel access requires a three-hour uphill hike or a ride on a century-old steam-powered train.

OPPOSITE: To celebrate the summer solstice, fires are lit along the mountains of the Zugspitz Arena in Ehrwald.

PAGES 160–161: Festival participants gather around bonfires along the Nordkette ridge above Innsbruck.

designated outpost and arrange hundreds of tiny torches to create the scene, then set them ablaze. As twilight descends, a full panorama of flickering mountainside motifs comes into view, creating a surreal summer kickoff that spectators can enjoy from a mountain perch or back down at sea level.

The best known bonfires glow atop the Tyrol's Ehrwald Basin, located in the region's Zugspitz Arena, a collection of seven towns on Austria's side of the Zugspitze mountain. The blazes here were inscribed to the UNESCO Intangible Cultural Heritage List in 2010. On a summer solstice visit, you can spot some 8,000 individual fires that roar around 6,560 feet (2,000 m) above sea level. Catch the cable car up from Ehrwald to admire the fiery arrangements head-on.

Innsbruck, capital of the Tyrol region, offers another cable-car perspective. Catch the gondola up to the Nordkette mountains for a close view of the flames, with mountaintop stargazing, music, and food on offer into the night.

Cruise Lake Achensee in the Tyrolean village of Pertisau, where the sky-high fires are reflected off glassy waters. Or admire the midsummer beauty via a boat ride along the Danube. The Wachau region in particular comes to life with floating lights, towering bonfires, and fireworks displays. A dinner and dancing Danube cruise aboard the M.S. *Wachau* from Melk provides an ideal post for soaking up the Austrian beauty—and don't be surprised if you're singing Julie Andrews's ode to Austria by the night's end.

BUNGEE AT DUSK

Add even more thrills with a free fall beneath the stars.

BUDGET: $$$ **WHEN TO GO:** May–October   **ACTIVITY LEVEL:** Strenuous   **GO FOR:** Adventure

I n 1995, James Bond put Switzerland's Verzasca Dam in the global spotlight. *GoldenEye* audiences around the world watched in awe as the famous 007 bungee jumped down the 721-foot (220 m) tall concrete dam to sneak into a Soviet weapons base.

In the film, this colossal slab of concrete was set in Russia. In reality, the dam overlooks Switzerland's Lago di Vogorno reservoir and is flanked by the jagged Swiss Central Alps. And it's not just world-renowned spies who can take the plunge. Today, the dam is a hub for bungee jumping—a feat you can try by day or, if you're extra daring, after dark.

The Verzasca Dam is among the highest bungee jumps in the world. It's also one of just a few places to offer nighttime free falls, available via outfitter 007Bungy. The reception and training area, as well as the jump platform, are well lit. Everything beyond that is pitch-dark. That means you'll soar through an inky abyss, seeing nothing but feeling everything—your heart in your throat, wind stretching your face, and your deafening scream echoing off the dam for some of the seemingly longest and wildest few seconds of your life.

Each trip begins with a jump training from the outfitter's safety professionals before stepping off the platform lip. The experience runs on select nights from May through October; check ahead for weather cancellations.

OPPOSITE: A plunge at the Verzasca Dam is an adrenaline rush by day—and even more thrilling after dark.

DARK SKY ALQUEVA RESERVE

See 286 clear nights a year at this certified astrotourism escape.

BUDGET: $ **WHEN TO GO:** Year-round   **ACTIVITY LEVEL:** Mild   **GO FOR:** Stargazing

Portugal's Dark Sky Alqueva Reserve is a playground for stargazers. The 3,800-square-mile (10,000 km²) amalgam of rolling hills and glassy lakes nabbed recognition as the world's first Starlight Tourism Destination in 2011, a certification granted by the UNESCO-supported Starlight Foundation. This European organization protects the darkness by engaging the public in astronomy, cultivating astrotourism experiences, and promoting stargazing-friendly lighting. Dark Sky Alqueva Reserve, which stretches from Portugal's Alentejo region into Spain, does all three, and then some.

The result: Some of the best nightscapes in western Europe, which are further enhanced by the region's minimal cloud cover. On average, Dark Sky Alqueva Reserve enjoys 286 clear, cloud-free nights each year.

The most popular stop for admiring the night sky is the reserve's observatory, located in the charming terra-cotta-roofed village of Cumeada. Guided nightscape experiences via telescopes and binoculars run almost daily, with a smorgasbord of interstellar sights from which to choose: planets, galaxies, nebulae, star clusters, and an up close glimpse of the moon. (During the day, guided experiences include safe solar observation.) Tours, available in English or Portuguese, require advanced reservations. In addition to exploring deep space, the observatory hosts special events, such as solar observation sessions accompanied by wine tastings from local vineyards, or astrophotography workshops.

WHERE TO STAY

Family-owned São Lourenço do Barrocal, a five-star resort in an ancient farming village, hosts private stargazing sessions in partnership with Dark Sky Alqueva. Astronomers lead discussions in the property's millennia-old bee garden and arena.

OPPOSITE: Venus rises on the horizon over a circle of standing stones in the Xerez Cromlech, a megalithic complex that dates back to the fourth or fifth millennium B.C.

PAGES 166–167: The Milky Way's core shines in brilliant color above Dark Sky Alqueva Reserve.

Astro-canoeing adds a touch of adventure to your stargazing escape. "It's a beautiful way to experience the night sky on Alqueva Lake," says Apolónia Rodrigues, founder and creator of Dark Sky Alqueva, noting the water's calm enough to see the stars twinkling both overhead and reflected below your canoe. Night canoeing runs from June through September.

Stargazing is even more humbling when you consider how early humans interpreted the cosmos. Dive deeper into this perspective with a trip to Neolithic Almendres Cromlech, an elliptical-shaped complex of ancient stone monuments placed approximately 8,000 years ago to predict the equinoxes and sun and moon cycles. This archaeoastronomy timekeeping tool predates England's Stonehenge; nearly all of the 100 original stone markers remain in place today. "These places testify to the importance of the sky to mankind, whether we're talking about today or a few millennia ago," Rodrigues says.

The reserve's growing list of after-dark experiences now includes guided night walks around Alqueva Lake, with stargazing and stories by the campfire, after-hours horseback rides on full-moon nights (or new-moon nights for experienced riders), and early morning hot-air balloon rides to catch first light from above. For the ultimate dose of awe, visit Dark Sky Alqueva Reserve during a new moon, when the skies are at their darkest. The Milky Way is most visible from May through September.

CEREMONY OF THE KEYS

Watch one of London's regal traditions at the Tower of London.

BUDGET: $ **WHEN TO GO:** Year-round **ACTIVITY LEVEL:** Mild **GO FOR:** Culture

More than 23,000 gemstones lie within the walls of the Tower of London, and the nightly Ceremony of the Keys has been in place for nearly seven centuries to protect them. The historic closing of the tower event welcomes some 50 spectators each night—and you can be among them.

Around 9:30 p.m., the ceremony leader and royal bodyguard, the Chief Yeoman Warder, greets guests at the tower gate. The warder, in his regal red waistcoat and top hat, explains the ceremony's history before the procession commences. Just after 9:50 p.m., the warder marches to the tower gate with a candle lantern in one hand and oversize keys in the other.

"Halt, who comes there?" the sentry calls.

"The keys," barks back the warder.

"Whose keys?" asks the sentry.

The warder then confirms the monarch's name. "Pass then," the sentry approves. "All's well."

In the past 700 years, the only deviation to this exchange has been the name of the monarch. The Ceremony of the Keys first began in the mid-1300s, when King Edward III waltzed into the tower unannounced, with no security in sight. He instituted the ritual in December 1340 to protect the crown jewels.

The ticketed event won't keep you out too late. It ends at exactly 10:05 p.m.

OPPOSITE: **It's an honor to be appointed Yeoman Gaoler, an ancient title created in the 16th century that is the second-in-command among the Yeomen Warders.**

ESTONIA

LAKE RUMMU NIGHT RAFTING

Float around a spooky Soviet-era prison complex.

BUDGET: $ **WHEN TO GO: April–May or August–November**   **ACTIVITY LEVEL: Intermediate**   **GO FOR: Adventure**

An eerie Soviet-era prison looms half-submerged above Estonia's Lake Rummu. See the haunting behemoth on a night paddle via a glowing raft tour with local outfitter Matkajuht.

On this dusky excursion around Lake Rummu and the now defunct Murru Prison, roughly 30 minutes east of Tallinn, you'll glide along the calm waters. The bottom of your raft is outfitted in lights that illuminate the former barracks and mazelike passageways below. These building remnants are part of a historic prison complex, erected in a former quarry around 1938. The prison was built as a working camp; under Soviet rule from 1940 to 1991, hundreds of inmates were forced to mine limestone for marble each day.

By the time Estonia gained its independence in 1991, the limestone supply had run dry and the prison was abandoned. Eventually, water from the lake seeped in and swallowed up most of Murru. The majority of the prison hides beneath the turquoise lake, except for portions of the dilapidated building and a few mining relics that pierce the water's surface.

Lights on your six-person raft unveil the former quarry's secrets and marvels. In addition to the prison remnants, you'll pass over a bewitching underwater forest, and see the schools of fish that inhabit it, throughout your two-hour float. Don't sleep on the daytime activities here, either, be it scuba diving among the prison remains or strolling by the lakeside dunes.

OPPOSITE: **A haunting sight: What's left of a former prison peeks out from the water of Lake Rummu.**

GREECE

FULL MOON FESTIVAL

Celebrate the August moon with extended museum hours.

BUDGET: $ **WHEN TO GO:** August   **ACTIVITY LEVEL:** Mild   **GO FOR:** Culture

With glowing monuments and star-splashed skies, the towns, peaks, and islands of Greece dazzle every night of the year. The celebration of August's full moon is a particular crowd-pleaser, though. It's an evening of song, dance, poem readings, and sightseeing, with more than 100 tourist spots throughout the country offering special—and often free—twilight events.

This lunar gaiety dates back millennia. Ancient Greeks used the August full moon, the brightest of the year, to celebrate the moon goddess, Selene. They even timed the earliest Olympic Games to this lunar spectacle.

Today, Greece continues to honor the August moon with a national festival that keeps its top archaeological sites and museums open well past dark.

In Athens, the Acropolis Museum plays host to after-hours entertainment, including live music and performances. Other city venues, such as the National Archaeological Museum and the Numismatic Museum courtyard, run twilight experiences, including late-night guided tours and concerts.

The Olympia archaeological site, the site of the original Olympic Games in western Peloponnese, is another worthwhile stop during the August celebration. Watch musicians perform traditional Greek tunes and dances, or stroll among temples and the world-renowned ancient stadium as the sacred sky beacon lights the way—just like it did thousands of years ago.

OPPOSITE: **In August, revelers across Greece celebrate the full moon, which rises majestically over ancient ruins, including Athens's Acropolis.**

EIFFEL TOWER ILLUMINATION

See the City of Light sparkle every hour, on the hour.

BUDGET: $ **WHEN TO GO:** Year-round   **ACTIVITY LEVEL:** Mild   **GO FOR:** Culture

Paris is always a good idea, especially at night. The City of Light shimmers beneath dark skies, with warmly lit icons like the Louvre and Notre-Dame Cathedral enchanting travelers as dusk descends. Of all the nighttime marvels, no Parisian light display is more lauded, or bookmarked, than the twinkling Eiffel Tower.

Every hour, on the hour, the iron icon erupts with five minutes of twinkling lights. The scene is so synonymous with Paris, it's hard to imagine a night in the city without it, yet the iconic iridescence is relatively new in the structure's more than 100 years of history.

In 1985, engineers installed hundreds of gold-hued lights on the tower. To celebrate the new millennium two decades later, mountain climbers fastened another 20,000 sparkling lights onto the tower. They removed the lights in 2001, then reinstalled them a year later along with tower-top spotlights to create a sweeping effect. The monument now sparkles for five minutes instead of 10 to save energy (an adjustment made in 2008). The last light show is at 11 p.m.; a steady gold glow illuminates the Eiffel Tower until 11:45 p.m.

You can soak up the splendor from one of many vantage points: the nearby Jardins du Trocadero, a Seine River cruise, and the overlook at Montparnasse Tower Panoramic Observation Deck. Or head to the tower's tippy top for a toast at the Eiffel Tower Champagne Bar, which serves bubbly until 11 p.m.

OPPOSITE: Seeing the Eiffel Tower sparkle at night is a quintessential Parisian experience.

A DARK SKY ISLAND

Discover a stargazing oasis in the English Channel.

BUDGET: $ **WHEN TO GO:** September–October   **ACTIVITY LEVEL:** Intermediate   **GO FOR:** Stargazing

On Sark, night sky protections take priority. The three-mile-long (5 km) English Channel island, population 600, has no streetlights or cars. The sole motorized vehicles that are allowed, tractors, must be off the road by 10 p.m. The result? Obsidian skies pierced by thousands of silvery pinpricks and such minimal light pollution you can spot the Milky Way from just about anywhere on the island. In 2011, light pollution authority DarkSky certified Sark as the world's first Dark Sky Island.

For an immersive night beneath the cosmos, book a visit to the Sark Astronomy Society's observatory. Volunteer guides lead by-appointment-only stargazing sessions to glimpse planets, constellations, and moon craters via a permanent 10-inch (25 cm) telescope.

Another starry outpost is La Coupée, a 262-foot (80 m) causeway that links the island with the "Little Sark" peninsula. This crag-meets-sea panorama wows around the clock—particularly when the Milky Way glimmers above, from late spring to early autumn.

For a full night of stargazing, snag a camping spot or glamping pod at family-run Pomme de Chien, located 10 minutes from town. The accommodation's wide-open fields promise sweeping sky views, whether you're spying on planets or hoping to catch a summer meteor shower, such as the Perseids.

To reach Sark, a protectorate of the United Kingdom in the English Channel, catch a boat from neighboring Channels Islands Guernsey or Jersey. September through October promise the best skygazing; you can spot stars in the summer, but from July to August, the nights have only about four hours of darkness.

OPPOSITE: Catch the sunset over the Corbière Lighthouse in Jersey, one of Sark's neighboring English Channel islands.

HALLOWEEN AT DRACULA'S CASTLE

Party at a haunted-season bash fit for the king of all vampires.

BUDGET: $$–$$$$ **WHEN TO GO:** October   **ACTIVITY LEVEL:** Mild   **GO FOR:** Culture

For a spine-tingling Halloween celebration, head to Dracula's Castle—rather, the real-life fortress readers most associate with the fictional vampire's abode. You'll find it in Bran, Romania.

Though Irish author Bram Stoker never stepped foot in Bran, many believe an illustration of the cliff-perched Bran Castle—the only real Transylvanian castle to fit Stoker's description—was the inspiration for Dracula's dwellings. The medieval fortress balances atop a 200-foot-tall (60 m) rock, flanked by verdant hills that spill to the horizon. Legend has it Stoker chose this region because of the infamous Vlad III Drăculea, known as Vlad the Impaler, a local warrior with a signature battle move: impaling his enemies with wood and metal stakes. An apt inspiration for Dracula himself.

The *Dracula* novel, published in 1897, catapulted bucolic Bran into pop culture. It now draws travelers with eerie legends, medieval attractions, and the ultimate event: an after-dark Halloween party in the famous Gothic castle. On the Saturday closest to Halloween, Bran Castle stays open after hours to welcome costumed revelers with night tours, a Romanian feast, and spooky holiday frivolity, including a special Halloween ride on the castle's renowned Time Tunnel—an animated glass elevator with ghosts, dragons, bats, and other haunts throughout its 60-second descent. The bash kicks off around 7:30 p.m.; tickets are required and sell out quickly.

OPPOSITE: Located just outside Brașov, Romania, Bran Castle is said to have been the inspiration for Dracula's castle in Bram Stoker's novel.

RIDE UNDER THE FULL MOON

Saddle up for a moonlit saunter through magical landscapes.

BUDGET: $$ **WHEN TO GO:** June–September   **ACTIVITY LEVEL:** Intermediate   **GO FOR:** Adventure

The Cappadocia region of Turkey (Türkiye) is a treat of topography. Volcanic tuffs rise above the cobblestone streets in historic villages like tourist hub Göreme, where homes, churches, and castles are carved deep into the hollowed-out rock. From Göreme to the horizon, it's a magical scene of fairy chimneys (dramatic hoodoo rock formations) and khaki-colored badlands under a sky peppered with hot-air balloons come first light.

Many hitch a ride on the colorful orbs to admire the region's fantastical landscapes, including Göreme National Park, a UNESCO World Heritage site. But there's another, authentically Cappadocian, way to soak up the views: on horseback. And during summer full moons, that may mean a horseback ride at dusk.

Horses are the backbone of the region's history. Around 1700 B.C., the Hittite Empire used horse-drawn chariots to battle enemies and gain power across Anatolia, present-day central Turkey. During the Ottoman Empire, roughly A.D. 1299 to 1922, equines were so prevalent that historical records say the sultan alone had 3,000 of them. For millennia, the region's farmers relied on horses to assist with agricultural labor. The brawny mammals pulled carts and plows during seasonal harvests; they were set free to scavenge for food each winter.

WHERE TO STAY

Don't just admire Cappadocia's dramatic cave dwellings; slumber in them. Museum Hotel, a Relais & Châteaux collection of historic and restored cave and stone houses decked with antiques and artwork, provides the ultimate Cappadocia overnight.

OPPOSITE: Your moonlit ride through the dramatic landscapes of Cappadocia begins at sunset.

PAGES 182-183: Fairy chimneys create a surreal, volcanic landscape throughout the Cappadocia region.

Over time, farming advancements reduced the need for horses, and local farmers eventually let their maned helpers roam the wilderness all year. The once domestic animals developed their own subset of undomesticated equines, known as *yılkı*, the term for a horse that's been released into nature. In some parts of Cappadocia, herds of yılkı have been thriving on their own for centuries. They're particularly prevalent on the slopes of Mount Erciyes, 63 miles (101 km) from Göreme.

On an after-dark horseback ride, you'll saddle tamed horses, not yılkı, though you'll learn about the latter on your trip. Local equestrian farms near Göreme and the otherworldly Göreme National Park—such as the Dalton Brothers Horse Ranch or Lucky Horse Ranch—offer summer excursions to watch the region's volcanic-morphed landforms shimmer beneath the full moon glow.

The tours travel far from light pollution, with a starlit and moonlit ride through tight passages; along cliffside caves, dungeons, and churches; and past erosion-carved pillars, which can reach up to 130 feet (40 m) tall. The equines don't need flashlights; instead, a bright full moon lights their way and the otherworldly surroundings, which are even more enchanting when paired with regional history narrated by the evening's guide.

Trips last for several hours and conclude with a campfire, traditional black Turkish tea (known as *çay*, pronounced like "chai"), and local wine. Tours run just before, on, and after the full moon, from June to September.

LONG NIGHT OF MUSEUMS

Wander galleries and exhibitions during a Berlin after-hours summer staple.

BUDGET: $ **WHEN TO GO:** August   **ACTIVITY LEVEL:** Mild   **GO FOR:** Culture

B erlin's Long Night of Museums has plenty of laid-back learning—and fun—to go around. Each year on the last Saturday of August, dozens of museums across the city keep their doors open well past dark. It's part of the decades-old Long Night of Museums festival, known locally as Langen Nacht der Museen. Berlin introduced the event in 1997 with a handful of extended-hours venues. A rave response pushed the city to repeat and expand the festivities. Now, around 70 museums and exhibition spaces across Berlin participate, with exhibits remaining open from around 6 p.m. to 2 a.m.

The Berlin mayor kicks off the night with a celebration at Lustgarten park on Museum Island, a UNESCO World Heritage site with five of the city's most popular venues, including the Pergamon Museum, an archaeological haven. Hundreds of after-hour exhibitions, special workshops, artist talks, cocktail hours, and music and dancing follow in museums throughout Berlin.

Explore staples like the art-packed Altes Museum, Berlin's first museum; the Bode Museum, known for its Byzantine art collection; or lesser known spaces that draw a fraction of the crowds. Off-the-beaten-path highlights include the German Spy Museum, the science-centric Futurium, the Stiftung Planetarium Berlin, and the Wilhelm Foerster Observatory, where telescopes let you spy on deep space happenings.

OPPOSITE: **Visit the Bode Museum, which opened to the public in 1904, for an after-dark tour through its magnificent collection of art and sculpture.**

ICE SHEET CAMPING

Spend an icy night above the Arctic Circle.

BUDGET: $$$ **WHEN TO GO:** March–October   **ACTIVITY LEVEL:** Strenuous   **GO FOR:** Adventure

---

Follow in the crampon-carved footsteps of polar explorers with a night of camping on the Greenland ice sheet. It's a rare and immersive way to admire the world's second largest expanse of ice, a blustery behemoth that blankets nearly 80 percent of Greenland's landmass with icy mountains, teal lakes, and a minefield of crevasses and moulins (deep shafts in the ice).

Given the harrowing surroundings, most overnight ice sheet jaunts are reserved for professional exploration or scientific research teams. But Camp Ice Cap makes the dream possible for more amateur, yet still intrepid, guests. The outfitter's two-day, one-night camping trip offers a taste of expedition life—but don't let the short duration fool you. A sleep on the unforgiving 656,000-square-mile (1.7 million km²) sheet of white—an expanse roughly the size of Alaska—is no walk in the park.

On the trip, you and a team of trekkers haul tents, sleeping bags, and fuel for roughly one hour of hiking into the ivory abyss. Once you reach your overnight accommodations—an open patch of ice—it's time to build camp from the ground up. You'll crank ice stakes, sort gear, pitch tents, and collect snow to boil for water.

It's grueling work, but the sweat's worth it for quality time with this rare wonder. Once camp is set, you'll have the opportunity to hike among ice mounds and pristine cerulean water bodies, aurora hunt (in the spring or fall), and admire the midnight sun come summer. Just as memorable are the deep conversations shared over freeze-dried dinners in Camp Ice Cap's orange

WHILE YOU'RE THERE

If a night at Camp Ice Cap whets your backcountry Greenland appetite, Kangerlussuaq has more where that came from. The town is connected to the island's famed Arctic Circle Trail, a 100-mile (160 km) thru-hike that runs from inland Kangerlussuaq to Sisimiut on the west coast. Expect unspoiled tundra sprinkled with musk oxen and reindeer on this roughly 10-day trek.

OPPOSITE: On the Greenland ice sheet, camping is chilly, but you'll find warmth wrapped in blankets under the midnight sun.

PAGES 188–189: Travelers can kayak, boat, or stand-up paddle through Greenland's many icefjords.

globe mess tent. One topic that's sure to arise among these fragile landscapes: climate change.

As the news headlines show, Greenland's ice sheet is ground zero of Earth's shifting climate. The white mass is expected to lose up to 110 trillion tons (100 trillion t) of ice by 2100—a change that could raise sea levels by a foot (30 cm). To do its part protecting this natural resource, Camp Ice Cap tour operator Albatros Arctic Circle has a strict Leave No Trace policy. That means everything you bring with you must be carried out.

Each season introduces a different flavor of adventure. Come in the calmer summer months for ice hikes with endless hours of daylight and, on the warmest days, even short dips in meltwater "lakes" (water temps hover slightly above freezing this time of year, but a warm sun can make the quick swim surprisingly refreshing). Visit in the shoulder seasons—spring or fall—for a chance to see auroras. But be prepared for particularly unpredictable and unforgiving weather

OTHER MARVELS

A quick 45-minute flight north from Kangerlussuaq will drop you in Ilulissat, home to the UNESCO World Heritage site Ilulissat Icefjord. This 34-mile (55 km) patchwork of icebergs, some 10 to 20 stories tall, stems from the Sermeq Kujalleq (also known as Jakobshavn Glacier), which runs from the Greenland ice sheet. It's one of the world's fastest-moving glaciers, and scientists believe it produced the fateful iceberg that struck the *Titanic* in 1912.

ABOVE: The northern lights, pictured here above Nuuk, are visible from September to April.

OPPOSITE: After camping, choose from various day-time activities, such as hiking.

that time of year. You could have a snowstorm, clear aurora-streaked skies, or both in the same night.

Weather is all part of the Camp Ice Cap adventure, as is the journey to get there in the first place. The trip begins in Kangerlussuaq, located inland in central-west Greenland. This town, home to one of the island's main international airports, has the only road in Greenland that connects to the ice sheet. It's a potholed 15.5-mile (25 km) route, with potential reindeer and musk ox sightings along the way.

A good base level of fitness is required for a Camp Ice Cap visit, as the hiking can be strenuous and requires a bit of agility on the ice.. Albatros Arctic Circle provides tents, sleeping bags, trekking poles, crampons, and food, but it's up to you to pack warm-weather essentials: coats, gloves, hats, wool layers, headlamps, and, by all means, an extra pair of socks.

WOLF SAFARI

Listen for howls in a moon-drenched woodland.

BUDGET: $$$ **WHEN TO GO:** July–September   **ACTIVITY LEVEL:** Intermediate   **GO FOR:** Wildlife

S eeing isn't always believing; that's something a Scandinavian wolf safari makes clear. These overnight expeditions, which run deep in the pine and spruce forests of central Sweden, focus on hearing, not spotting, the elusive canines. "We sit in the dark forest silently and wait for hours before we hear the howl," says Marcus Eldh, founder and owner of WildSweden, the outfitter behind the region's gray wolf safaris. Taking an auditory approach lets the animals move about undisturbed.

The summer trips commence near the town of Färna, a two-hour drive northwest of Stockholm. On your hike into wolf country, you'll pad among thick evergreens and bone white birches, scanning the forest floor for wolf clues—paw prints, droppings, or left-behind prey.

Each outing, run in collaboration with the Scandinavian Wolf Research Project, a conservation organization, includes experienced guides and local researchers who share wolf knowledge with you, including background on the species' current threats (such as deforestation and poaching) and their comeback story, which was aided by community and scientific efforts. In the 1960s, scientists believed the creatures had gone extinct in Sweden. Then, in the 1980s, a handful of Russian-Finnish wolves migrated to Sweden. The animals migrated in solitude, often searching for new territories or partners, says Eldh. As luck would have it, a male and female migrated to and met in the same area of Sweden in 1983. The Scandinavian population has since rebounded to more than 300 wolves.

OPPOSITE: **More than 300 gray wolves now live in Sweden, a species comeback story.**

PAGES 194-195: **Come winter, Sweden is also ideal for northern lights viewing— especially on clear nights.**

Another topic of conversation is why wolves howl in the first place. Wolves call to gather troops for hunting, warn nearby pack members of danger, or challenge canines from other groups. When multiple wolves howl at once, known as a chorus howl, it can alert other packs or lone wolves to avoid their territory.

After setting up camp and enjoying a fire-cooked meal, you'll follow the guides even deeper into the woods to listen. Once seated on the woodland floor, get ready to perk your ears and pay attention to the forest. A call could come at any time. "The silence is an important part of the experience," says Eldh, noting that canines aren't the only ones that communicate under inky skies and between trees. You could hear tawny owls, nightjars, and grasshoppers as you wait for the canines.

After minutes or hours of anticipation and silent meditation, the majestic wolf howl echoing through the woodlands can prove powerful enough to bring guests to tears, says Eldh. "It makes people feel primitive and close to nature."

FAST FACT

Despite common folklore, wolves don't actually howl at the moon—but they do howl toward it. The canines point their heads upward when calling out because the acoustics help their sounds travel farther, up to six miles (10 km) in the forest and 10 miles (16 km) in open terrain.

For a different perspective, take in the sweeping Grand Canyon at dusk or dawn—or sleep on the canyon floor (page 274).

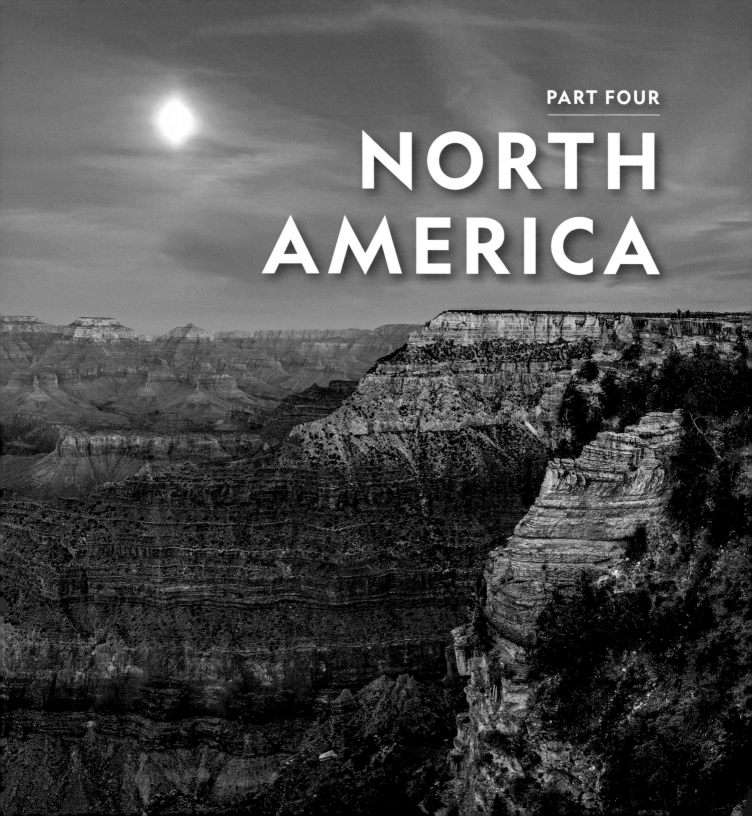

PART FOUR

NORTH AMERICA

IGLOO OVERNIGHTS

Build, then snooze in, an authentic Arctic abode.

BUDGET: $$$$ **WHEN TO GO:** December–April   **ACTIVITY LEVEL:** Intermediate   **GO FOR:** Adventure

The igloo is an architectural marvel. Its construction is part science, part art—and a whole lot of work. You can learn the millennia-old building method and make your own snow shelter, then sleep in it, with a night at Okpik Arctic Village, an Arctic getaway in Canada's Northwest Territories. "Spending the night in an igloo is one of the closest things to getting in a time machine," says Kylik Kisoun Taylor, founder of Tundra North Tours and Okpik Arctic Village, which is located on an island in the Mackenzie River, around 20 minutes by boat from Inuvik. "It gives a lot of perspective, and a respect for the [Inuit] people and the culture."

Throughout history, Inuit people (the Indigenous communities from the Arctic regions of Canada, Greenland, Alaska, and Russia) built igloos for protection from harsh winters. They stacked blocks of compressed snow into a dome-shaped structure, built around a hole in the frozen ground. A small vent in the dome's top lets smoke from the evening fire escape. Snow, not ice, proved to be the best building material. "Snow has an insulating factor, and it can definitely be warm," says Taylor, noting "warm" is relative in the Northwest Territories' below-freezing winters.

As technologies advanced, Inuit hunters moved away from igloos, opting for easier on-the-go shelters, such as tents. "My family had lost those skills," says Taylor, who's one-quarter Inuvialuit (western Canadian Inuit) and one-quarter Gwich'in (among the northernmost Indigenous peoples, living from interior Alaska through the Yukon territory and Mackenzie Valley in Canada). Instead of learning the igloo-building craft from his elders, Taylor

OTHER MARVELS

After weeks without sunlight in December, Inuvik embraces daylight's return with the annual Inuvik Sunrise Festival in January. Merrymaking includes traditional food, dance, and cultural workshops, with igloos on display and fireworks to cap off the fanfare.

OPPOSITE: Traditional igloos are built from packed snow, not ice, which helps keep inhabitants warmer and more insulated from weather.

PAGES 200-201: With traditional survival tools nearby, an Inuit woman inspects a handsewn boot.

searched online. He and a friend watched step-by-step videos, then not only built their own igloo, but started teaching others in the community, including their elders. "It's a transfer of knowledge going the opposite way," he says.

After spreading igloo-building knowledge with the community in Inuvik, Taylor coordinated trips to share this tradition with travelers. He sees tourism as a way to keep the craft alive.

Okpik Arctic Village's igloo-building immersion, which runs from December through April, begins with a daytime demonstration. You'll learn the history of these snow-packed abodes, then you and your fellow guests will work together to build one of your own. Construction can take a full day. "It's a lot like art," says Taylor. "There's no blueprint, so each block is different."

Travelers with limited time—or minimal cold tolerance—can place a few snowy bricks, then head inside for tea or another activity. Winter experiences at Okpik Arctic Village run the gamut: snowshoeing, skiing, fat-tire biking, fishing, traditional cooking demonstrations, and hanging with resident sled dogs.

Come nightfall, you'll join local and Indigenous guides for storytelling and potential northern lights sightings by the fire. Then, it's time to sleep in the masterpiece you, or the Okpik team, built by hand. It's a traditional, teeth-chattering experience, but you will have a handful of luxuries to keep you warm, such as caribou hide, a *kudlik* (oil lamp), and sleeping bags.

MIDNIGHT SUN PADDLING

Spend a sun-drenched midnight on the history-steeped Yukon River.

BUDGET: $–$$$ **WHEN TO GO:** May–July   **ACTIVITY LEVEL:** Intermediate to strenuous   **GO FOR:** Adventure

History trickles through the Yukon River, an almost 2,000-mile (3,220 km) waterway that links northwestern Canada, then Alaska, with the Bering Sea. The nearly 450-mile (720 km) Canadian stretch from Whitehorse to Dawson City is particularly legendary. Thousands of prospectors tackled this route to find their fortunes during the Klondike gold rush in the late 1800s.

The annual Yukon River Quest kicks off summer and memorializes this prospecting heritage with an around-the-clock kayak and canoe race, typically in early July. Paddlers from across the globe flock to the starting point, downtown Whitehorse, the capital city of Canada's Yukon. They spend day and night racing beneath the midnight sun to reach Dawson City, located 444 miles (715 km) away.

It's a hair-raising race spanning multiple days along the river's untamed boreal forests. The record is just under 40 hours, although this trip typically takes paddlers more than two weeks to complete. The experience is also an immersion into the region's dazzling 24 hours of sun. "The light is different, the sounds are different," says Kalin Pallett, president of the Wilderness Tourism Association of the Yukon, noting that, during the midnight sun, high-noon brightness doesn't even hit until the evening. "The sun just bounces along the horizon and never fully sets."

FAST FACT

Every year, Canada's Yukon welcomes the longest land migration on Earth, the migration of the Porcupine caribou. Some 200,000 of the ungulates follow food sources more than 745 miles (1,200 km) from the boreal forests of the Northwest and Yukon Territories and Alaska into the Arctic coastal plain.

OPPOSITE: Twenty-four hours of daylight means you can paddle the Yukon River well past your bedtime.

PAGES 204-205: The Yukon River winds for 1,980 miles (3,190 km) from British Columbia into the Yukon.

Paddling the Yukon is also a chance to meet and learn about the Indigenous communities that live along this waterway. The stretch of river from Whitehorse to Dawson City passes by the territories of five First Nations communities who have been traveling the corridor for millennia, using the waterway for transportation and trade.

If you'd prefer a mild midnight sun paddle over a multiday race, options are aplenty. Tour outfitters throughout the region run midnight sun–timed overnight, long weekend, and multiweek trips. You'll paddle from day into night, then sleep on the riverbanks—or at least attempt to—beneath the shimmery sun. The spruces, pines, and aspens that dot the waterway provide a sense of calm, while potential wildlife sightings, from moose to bears to bald eagles, promise even more thrills.

No matter your paddle experience, you'll find a Yukon waterway to fit your skill level, says Pallett. "We have small lakes with good fishing, big lakes that get rowdy like the ocean, flat-water rivers, and Class IV whitewater."

May to September are the best months for late-night Yukon River paddling outside of race time. The region experiences 24 hours of daylight from mid-May to July. Visit in late June or early July for the annual Adäka Cultural Festival in Whitehorse. This celebration of Northern Dene Nations and Yukon First Nations features traditional music, stories, artwork, history, and panels on Indigenous languages.

A STARGAZING TRAM

Look to the sky as you ride to the top of Jasper's mountains.

BUDGET: $$ **WHEN TO GO:** September–October   **ACTIVITY LEVEL:** Mild   **GO FOR:** Stargazing

Soar closer to the cosmos on a star-studded night in the middle of Canada's Rocky Mountains. Your vessel, the Jasper SkyTram, holds the record for Canada's longest and highest guided aerial tramway. Over the course of seven minutes, the cable car flies from the base station near Marmot Basin ski resort to high above Jasper National Park's steep crags and pine-carpeted valleys, ultimately reaching the Whistlers Mountain upper station at an elevation of 7,424 feet (2,263 m) above sea level.

It's a scenic jaunt at any hour, but fall's special-edition stargazing rides enhance the view. On weekend nights from September into October, the SkyTram becomes a portal to the galaxy, and one of many venues for interstellar sightseeing inside Jasper National Park, a Dark Sky Preserve certified by the Royal Astronomical Society in Canada.

Your evening Jasper SkyTram trip starts with a 15-minute night sky orientation in an inflatable planetary dome at the cable-car base, located about four miles (7 km) from downtown Jasper. With astronomical intel under your belt, you'll board your pseudo-spacecraft and climb heavenward, watching stars and planets as they near by the second.

At the upper station, just 656 feet (200 m) from the Whistlers Mountain summit, the Jasper Planetarium crew will point out planets, galaxies, and nebulae through some of the most powerful telescopes in the Rockies.

OPPOSITE: Passengers on the Jasper SkyTram have uninterrupted views of the night sky and a chance to spot the Milky Way above Mount Andromeda and Mount Athabasca.

MIDNIGHT SUN BASEBALL GAME

Play ball during this late-night game of America's favorite pastime.

BUDGET: $ **WHEN TO GO:** June   **ACTIVITY LEVEL:** Mild   **GO FOR:** Culture

Nothing screams summer like peanuts and Cracker Jack, but Fairbanks, Alaska, takes America's favorite pastime one step further: a late-night baseball game beneath the midnight sun. This century-old tradition coincides with June's summer solstice. Teams play solely by the glow of the midnight sun, no stadium lights needed. It's a bucket-list night for sports fans, but it may require coffee. The first pitch of the Midnight Sun Baseball Game isn't thrown until 10 p.m.

Fairbanks, aka the land of the midnight sun, lies just 140 miles (225 km) from the Arctic Circle. It's one of the best U.S. getaways to experience the discombobulating 24 hours of daylight, from late April to late August.

In 1906, two local Fairbanks bars introduced the idea of a midnight sun ball game. More than 100 years later, the minor-league game is still going strong. It has welcomed opponents from around the world, as well as Hall of Famers like Tom Seaver and Dave Winfield.

You can catch the event at the 3,500-person Growden Memorial Park, home to the Alaska Goldpanners. As the home team tosses the first pitch, the sun nears the horizon, but it never sets during the game. It provides so much light, the stadium doesn't need to turn on their overheads. The seventh-inning stretch typically hits around midnight. To welcome the new day, fans belt "Alaska's Flag," the state song, during the half inning closest to 12 a.m.

OPPOSITE: **At the 113th Midnight Sun Game, the Orange County Surf play the Alaska Goldpanners at Growden Memorial Park in Fairbanks, Alaska.**

CUMBERLAND FALLS MOONBOW

View surreal lunar rainbows at the Niagara of the South.

BUDGET: $ **WHEN TO GO:** Year-round   **ACTIVITY LEVEL:** Mild   **GO FOR:** Nature

There's a twilight treat waiting among the white pines and hemlocks of Kentucky's Daniel Boone National Forest. The state's seven-story Cumberland Falls, nicknamed the Niagara of the South and located between Lexington, Kentucky, and Knoxville, Tennessee, is one of only a few waterfalls in the country with the right conditions to create a moonbow.

Unlike a typical rainbow, which forms its colors from sunlight hitting moisture in the air, the lunar version gets its glow from the bright full moon. The moon is 400,000 times less powerful than the sun, so moonbows are fainter than your daytime colorful rainbows. To the naked eye, they appear more like an ethereal white. Use a DSLR or mirrorless camera, or even a long-exposure app on your smartphone to see the hues pop.

The appearance of a moonbow requires near-perfect conditions, and Cumberland Falls checks each box: It generates a prolific spray, the area has minimal light pollution, its low gorge walls don't obstruct the moonlight, and the viewing area positions the moon at your back. Weather is the only gamble; you need minimal cloud cover to see the arc.

Winter tends to produce the best moonbows, but you can catch it year-round on full-moon nights. The upper viewing deck, accessible via a short walk from the visitors center parking lot, provides the best vantage point.

OPPOSITE: Cumberland Falls is one of the few spots around the world that regularly produces a moonbow.

UTAH, UNITED STATES

FULL-MOON HIKE

Explore Arches National Park by moonlight.

BUDGET: $ **WHEN TO GO:** May–September **ACTIVITY LEVEL:** Intermediate **GO FOR:** Adventure

With twinkling stars and soaring sandstone, a twilight hike in Arches National Park feels like teleporting to outer space—especially on a full-moon night. When the moon is at its fullest, sans clouds, it's brilliant enough to illuminate your way among the park's imposing arches and rust-hued rock fins. "It feels like not only are you walking by the moonlight, but you yourself are on the moon," says Arches National Park ranger Kait Thomas.

A full-moon hike is also a smart way to see one of the country's most visited national parks without heavy crowds. Arches remains open 24 hours a day, 365 days a year. The bulk of visitors come by daylight; after dusk, you'll see a fraction of the daytime crowds. And options abound for hitting Arches' myriad trails after dark.

A three-mile (4.8 km) round-trip hike provides a close-up view of Delicate Arch, the largest of the park's roughly 2,000 arches. The freestanding red giant, which creates a 46-foot-tall (14 m) window, looks otherworldly beneath the moon's glow. Beware, though: Delicate Arch takes a bit of know-how and stamina, particularly at night. Drop-offs and rock cracks create a minefield of hazards en route to the arch's base. The path also gains around 500 feet (152 m) of elevation. If you're trekking at night, it's wise to first familiarize yourself with the route by day. An alternative Delicate Arch perspective, the vista from Upper Viewpoint, is reachable via a half-mile (0.8 km) climb up stairs.

Another full-moon showstopper: the park's Windows Section, where a

OPPOSITE: The Milky Way appears above Utah's famous Delicate Arch, a 52-foot-tall (16 m) natural arch in Arches National Park.

PAGES 214-215: The full moon illuminates Turret Arch.

collection of unearthly rock fins, spires, and the namesake North and South Windows—two linked arches with punched-out centers—line up like a curated geology exhibit. "These are such unlikely formations," Thomas says of the site's number of arches. "And here are half a dozen and you can see them all at once." The one-mile (1.6 km) trail beneath the Windows is significantly flatter than Delicate Arch. If you time it just right, you may even catch the moon peeking through the North Window arch like an evil eye.

The 2.3-mile (3.7 km) Broken Arch Loop Trail around Sand Dune Arch provides another moderate, eye-popping night jaunt. You'll amble among canyons and boulders on your way to Broken Arch, a less visited stone formation that overlooks a patchwork of piñon and juniper trees below.

While you're in the park, the full moon is often bright enough to light your path, but it's important to pack ample illumination gear, such as flashlights or headlamps, in case the clouds descend. Opt for red-light lamps to avoid disrupting

WHERE TO STAY

There's one campground in Arches National Park, Devils Garden, and it's reservation-only during peak season. For an alternative that's a touch more pampered, try nearby Under Canvas, a Moab glamping site in the desert with unobstructed skies, nightly fire pits and s'mores, and stargazing from your pre-pitched tent's front patio.

ABOVE: **If you can score a night camping in the park, make sure to wake before sunset for one-of-a-kind views.**

OPPOSITE: **The rock art found throughout Arches National Park is believed to be 1,500 to 4,000 years old.**

wildlife, and wear closed-toe shoes for safety. Though Arches does remain open year-round, the months between spring and fall are best; winter's ice can make night hikes extra dicey.

A shimmering full moon isn't the only reason to visit Arches after dark. The park's stargazing is equally out of this world. In 2019, Arches earned its certification as a Dark Sky Park from DarkSky International, the global authority on light pollution. Skies here get black enough to see the Milky Way, along with views of star clusters without the need for telescopes. Some of the most unobstructed vantage points to take in night sky panoramas include Balanced Rock Picnic Area (which also boasts spectacular views of the Salt Valley), the Windows Section (also a great spot to catch a sunset), and the Garden of Eden viewpoint. If your heart's set on stargazing, try to time your visit to a new-moon night for the darkest skies and brightest celestial sights.

NIGHT SKIING

Extend a day on the slopes with an after-dark run.

BUDGET: $-$$ **WHEN TO GO:** December–March   **ACTIVITY LEVEL:** Intermediate   **GO FOR:** Adventure

Imagine zipping down freshly groomed powder with a starry sky—and a border of ski lights—illuminating your way. For many, night skiing is an added thrill to an already fun day on the slopes. It's the chance to keep the adrenaline pumping after hours, and to see the trails in a different light, literally. To partake, head to Steamboat Springs, home to two of Colorado's best night-ski escapes, not to mention some of the region's best snow.

World-class Steamboat Ski Resort intermittently runs three hours of night skiing from late December through March every Thursday through Sunday (outside of holidays). On these trails, you won't get the sloppy seconds of daytime skiers. Crews groom the trails each evening, before the after-dark slopes open, typically around 5:30 p.m. Snag a chairlift up the 8,000-foot (2,440 m) Christie Peak and catch one of five illuminated routes. The runs, which vary from beginner to advanced, send you gliding down 1,100 vertical feet (335 m) with Yampa Valley and Steamboat Springs's illuminated downtown in the distance.

Howelsen Hill, Colorado's oldest continually operating ski area, offers night runs Monday to Friday, typically between 5 and 8 p.m. Nearly 90 Olympians have used the area as their practice grounds, but the park also has three worthwhile stretches open for night skiing: the Face, Wren's Run, and Pony Land.

Make sure to pack extra layers and use goggles with lighter lenses than your daytime specs, such as yellow, for visibility.

OPPOSITE: Take on Steamboat Ski Resort's Christie Peak with five illuminated night routes.

GREAT LAKES NORTHERN LIGHTS

Watch the aurora borealis without leaving the contiguous United States.

BUDGET: $ **WHEN TO GO: Year-round**   **ACTIVITY LEVEL: Mild**   **GO FOR: Aurora chasing**

You don't have to globe-trot to Iceland or Finland for a dreamy night beneath the northern lights. When aurora activity is strong enough, you can catch those swirling viridian streaks along the border of the United States and Canada (and sometimes even farther south). Northern Minnesota, in particular, promises stellar aurora odds, and we have the North Pole's geomagnetic tilt to thank for that.

"If you look at the auroral oval [the path of the aurora's movements], it's always tilted more closely toward the top of Minnesota," says astrophotographer Mike Shaw, founder of the Great Lakes region's annual Aurora Summit. "It's scientifically the best place in the continental U.S. to see it." That said, hunting the aurora borealis in the lower 48 states is trickier than in polar regions. It requires a strong solar storm, good weather, minimal light pollution, and the right viewpoint.

First up: solar storm intensity. Storms on the sun fling solar winds packed with charged particles toward Earth's atmosphere. The collision between these electrons and protons and our planet's protective layers creates the aurora's dreamy, kaleidoscopic nightscapes.

The stronger the solar storm, the more vibrant the light show and the more likely you are to see it in lower latitudes, like in Minnesota. You can monitor storm intensity with apps like SpaceWeatherLive. Metrics like the

OPPOSITE: **On northern Minnesota nights, keep an eye on the sky—the aurora borealis can appear any month of the year.**

PAGES 222-223: **The northern lights appear on the horizon because of the Great Lakes region's distance from Earth's magnetic poles.**

Kp-index, a measure of disruptions in Earth's magnetic field, and Bz, the magnetic orientation of the solar winds, are key. The Kp range runs from 0 to 9. The higher the number, the farther south the auroras may travel. If you see Kp 4 or higher in northern Minnesota, with a negative Bz, it's time to head outside.

A good rule of thumb? If you can see the stars, you can technically see the auroras. But you'll also need dark skies with limited light pollution for a clear view. For that, try Boundary Waters Canoe Area Wilderness, certified as a DarkSky International Dark Sky Sanctuary, or Voyageurs National Park, another certified Dark Sky Park. Both remote, far north escapes are part of the Heart of the Continent Dark Sky Initiative, an international collaboration with Canada to protect nightscapes.

These two dark sky destinations also have minimal obstructions to the north horizon. When the sun's particles interact with Earth's atmosphere, the reactions occur near our planet's poles. In polar regions, where the collisions occur, the lights often dance overhead. In lower-latitude

ASTRONOMICAL WONDERS

The sun is the catalyst for Earth's dazzling aurora displays. It runs through 11-year activity periods, known as solar cycles. During low activity, solar minimum, you'll see few aurora displays. The peak, solar maximum, generates stronger sun storms and a boom in aurora activity. The next solar maximum is expected to hit around 2025, then again roughly a decade later.

ABOVE: For the best chance at seeing the northern lights, choose a vantage point in a DarkSky-certified destination.

OPPOSITE: Colors abound as the aurora swirls in green, red, pink, and blue.

spots like Minnesota, the reaction you're seeing is typically hundreds or thousands of miles away. That means the ribbons here often sashay closer to the horizon line.

Overlooks with open views to the north, such as mountaintops or large lakes, provide the best vantage point. As the Land of 10,000 Lakes, Minnesota is blessed with the latter, particularly across its DarkSky International–certified destinations. Other aurora-hunting hot spots in the Great Lakes region include Apostle Islands National Lakeshore in Wisconsin and the Keweenaw Peninsula in Michigan's Upper Peninsula.

It may be tougher to catch auroras in the contiguous United States than in the Arctic, but there is one advantage: year-round chasing. Unlike polar regions, where summer's midnight sun conceals auroras from roughly June through late August, Minnesota enjoys nighttime darkness all year.

YOOPERLITE SCOUTING

Search for glowing rocks on Michigan's shores.

BUDGET: $$-$$$ **WHEN TO GO:** July-September   **ACTIVITY LEVEL:** Intermediate   **GO FOR:** Nature

M
ichigan's far-flung Upper Peninsula (UP), the northernmost stretch of the state, brims with natural beauty, from craggy sandstone cliffs and Milky Way–splashed skies to the glow-in-the-dark stones that send rock hounds on twilight treasure hunts all summer long.

These vibrant rocks, nicknamed Yooperlites, are coarse gray syenite rocks that contain the mineral sodalite, which fluoresces under UV light. (Officially, the rocks are known as fluorescent sodalite-bearing syenite.) By day, the igneous rubble looks like your average stone. Come nightfall, beneath a UV glow, sodalite absorbs the light, then emits it in another wavelength. The result: a stone flecked with tangerine streaks that looks like something from *Alice in Wonderland*—not a stone on the shores of northern Michigan.

Scientists believe Yooperlites stem from magma some 1.1 billion years ago. Glaciers from the last ice age scooped the syenite rocks out from underground in present-day Canada, then scattered them across the Laurentian Plateau (the Canadian continental shield) and across the Great Lakes, particularly in Michigan.

The stone gets its nickname from a term for UP residents, known as Yoopers. Though Yooperlites are most common in Michigan, particularly along the rocky shores of the far north Keweenaw Peninsula and Grand Marais, you

OPPOSITE: Yooperlites glow under UV light, almost as if they're on fire.

PAGES 228-229: Scour the shores of the Keweenaw Peninsula for Yooperlites, among other rocky treasures.

can spot them across the whole of the Great Lakes region's pebble-dashed shores.

You'll need specific gear to find these glowing rocks, including a filtered 365-nanometer UV light, a headlamp or flashlight for safety, and sturdy shoes that can get wet. To improve your odds, join an expert-led rock tour, which will also provide the necessary equipment. Michigander Erik Rinta-maki, the first to find and report on the state's Yooperlites in 2017, now leads after-dark excursions to help visitors spot these stunners in the UP.

You can see the rocks any time of year, but timing your glow-in-the-dark adventure for late spring, summer, or early fall is best; Michigan winters gets cold, dark, and icy. Spring, when ice and snow have shifted the rocks, is particularly promising.

Though keeping your eyes on the ground is tempting, make a point to look up. Northern Michigan has some of the darkest, most star-drenched skies in the state—perfect for gazing at meteor showers, the Milky Way, and, on the luckiest nights, swirling auroras.

WHERE TO STAY

Don't look for Yooperlites just anywhere; sleep within steps of them at Fresh Coast Cabins, a family-owned escape on Michigan's far north Keweenaw Peninsula. At this collection of hip and upcycled cabins on Lake Superior's rock-strewn shore, you can search for Yooperlites—and the northern lights—right from your waterfront porch or the lake-view Finnish sauna.

CALIFORNIA, UNITED STATES

HOLLYWOOD FOREVER FILMS

Catch a flick at a star-studded cemetery in Tinseltown.

BUDGET: $ **WHEN TO GO:** May–September   **ACTIVITY LEVEL:** Mild   **GO FOR:** Culture

Every summer, Los Angeles' palm-strewn Hollywood Forever Cemetery morphs into a bustling open-air movie theater. Thousands flock to its lawn to watch their favorite big-screen stars beneath the stars, with food, photo booths, and DJ-spun dance parties to follow.

The backdrop for this outdoor cinema series, known as Cinespia, is an icon in and of itself. The Hollywood Forever Cemetery was erected in 1899 and joined the National Register of Historic Places in 1999. It's the final resting place for renowned Tinseltown actors and artists such as Judy Garland and Burt Reynolds. The cemetery occupies 62 acres (25 ha) of central Hollywood, and Hollywood Walk of Fame is just a mile (1.6 km) north.

Cinespia's Saturday night entertainment runs on the cemetery's grassy (and grave-free) Fairbanks Lawn. Projected movies flicker across an ivory-hued mausoleum, as patrons lounge and snack on a sea of picnic blankets. You can bring your own food, beer, and wine, although bites are also available from the snack bar. The night starts with some natural magic—sunset over the cemetery. Then, the show officially begins.

The event, which runs every Saturday evening and select Fridays between May and September, sells out most nights. Weather permitting, the screenings continue into October with Halloween flicks. Purchase tickets in advance; seating is available on a first-come, first-served basis.

OPPOSITE: As a Hollywood rite of passage, catch a famous flick in a cemetery that serves as the final resting place of cinema's elite.

TIMES SQUARE'S BALL DROP

Ring in the New Year in the heart of Manhattan.

BUDGET: $ **WHEN TO GO:** December 31 **ACTIVITY LEVEL:** Mild **GO FOR:** Culture

New York City's Times Square is so bright astronauts can see its shine from space. And no night is more synonymous with Midtown's glittery lights and frenetic energy than New Year's Eve.

Every December 31, around a million celebrators cluster in the heart of Manhattan for the New Year's Eve extravaganza. Live music, dancing, and frivolity set the stage for a grand finale millions around the world tune in to see: the 60-second ball drop atop the One Times Square skyscraper. A confetti canon and "Auld Lang Syne" fill the air once the glistening sphere completes its journey. Down at ground level, loved ones smooch, embrace, and dream about the year ahead.

It's a century-old tradition. Before signmaking firm Artkraft Strauss designed the first ball in 1907, hundreds of thousands of New Yorkers and visitors gathered cheek to jowl in Midtown Manhattan near the New York Times Building (One Times Square today) to watch the sky fill with fireworks at the stroke of midnight. The show captivated spectators, but pyrotechnics above a crowded NYC street proved unsafe—hot ash remnants sprinkled across the concrete jungle by the dawn of the New Year.

After several of those hazardous years, it was time for a fresh—and safer— New Year's Eve tradition. In due time, the ball drop came into play. The concept stemmed from 19th-century nautical devices. Harbor workers at

FAST FACT

The NYC ball has dropped annually since its first 1907 plunge, with the exception of two years: 1942 and 1943, when, following the Pearl Harbor attacks, the city dimmed its lights to hide and protect its highly distinguishable skyline.

OPPOSITE: Arrive hours early for a spot in Times Square to watch the crystal-covered ball drop at midnight.

PAGES 234-235: An estimated one million people celebrate New Year's Eve together in Times Square, while more than a billion around the world watch the ball drop from home.

that time lifted and lowered metal balls every day to help sailors sync their navigation instruments. The Times Square Ball, originally a 700-pound (320 kg) iron and wood behemoth, made its first drop in 1907, lowered from the One Times Square skyscraper. After half a dozen redesigns, today's bedazzled giant, introduced in 2007, weighs 11,875 pounds (5,386 kg) and impresses with thousands of Waterford crystal triangles. It's displayed above One Times Square year-round.

The 1970s introduced another new addition to the December 31 festivities: television personality Dick Clark. His *New Year's Rockin' Eve* began airing on NBC in 1972 (then on ABC from 1974 onward) and officially put the Times Square celebration—and his countdown to it—on the world stage.

Entrance to Times Square for the ball drop is free to the public. The thoroughfare is divided into a maze of corrals and blocked off for pedestrians only. Space—standing room only—is available first come, first served. The ball lift and the New Year's Eve entertainment (concerts, celebrity guests, and more) begin at 6 p.m. Experts recommend arriving in the early afternoon to snag a spot. Given the square doesn't have public bathrooms, some celebrators even wear diapers to the event. For a more luxurious start to the year, grab tickets to a ball-drop watch party in nearby venues, such as the Hyatt Centric Times Square hotel or the Marriott Marquis Times Square, which overlook the excitement with views of the ball drop.

DRIVE-IN MOVIE

Park the car for a nostalgic date night.

BUDGET: $ **WHEN TO GO:** Year-round   **ACTIVITY LEVEL:** Mild   **GO FOR:** Culture

Few nighttime activities embody Americana like catching a flick at a drive-in theater. To partake, head to Lehigh County, Pennsylvania, home of the country's oldest operating cinema of its kind: Shankweiler's Drive-In Theatre.

The facility, erected in 1934, was among the earliest drive-in venues in America. Today, movie buffs still enjoy blockbuster hits and nostalgic throwbacks via Shankweiler's year-round entertainment and nightly double features. Yet an evening at this Pennsylvania icon goes beyond catching an outdoor flick. For many, Shankweiler's is a drive down memory lane.

The nearly century-old venue was modeled after the country's first patented drive-in theater, Camden Drive-In in New Jersey, which opened in 1933. The concept, in general, was the brainchild of New Jersey native Richard Hollingshead, who wanted a new, more comfortable way to watch a movie without cramming into cinema seats. His first theater was a makeshift drive-in, projecting a film from his car and onto his home garage. Hollingshead's mom was guest number one. He quickly realized the potential, then turned the concept into a reality with Camden Drive-In. Its success led to thousands of other automobile entertainment venues around the country.

During the drive-in boom of the 1950s and 1960s, the United States had about 4,000 of these theaters, largely in rural areas. Societal changes, from shifting entertainment technology to downsized cars, have turned many of the venues into relics. Only some 300 drive-ins remain; the majority are in New York, Pennsylvania, and Ohio.

WHILE YOU'RE THERE

Drive-in by night, hike by day. Shankweiler's Drive-In Theatre is just a 20-minute drive south from eastern Pennsylvania's stretch of the Appalachian Trail. Take on part of it, starting at the Lehigh Gap Nature Center.

OPPOSITE: Park the car for a taste of nostalgia—a movie night at the drive-in.

PAGES 238-239: Shankweiler's Drive-In Theatre is the oldest operating drive-in theater in the United States.

Shankweiler's Drive-In Theatre, located just outside Allentown, Pennsylvania, has survived several iterations and renovations, including after major damage from 1955's Hurricane Diane. In the 1980s, it made history as the first drive-in theater to transmit a film's audio via FM broadcast stereo. Though the venue has adopted modern digital projection, visitors still tune into 90.7 FM to hear the movie.

Shankweiler's remains the most historic place to saddle up for a night of classic American entertainment, with nostalgic treats like funnel cakes, ice-cream sandwiches, and cotton candy at the snack bar. But it's not the only place to enjoy movie-night nostalgia. The Wellfleet, one of the last drive-ins on Cape Cod, Massachusetts, is among the East Coast's most famed drive-in haunts. Watch the latest hits in this 1957 theater, and pair date night with on-site mini golf.

In the Catskills region of New York, the Greenville Drive-in draws movie buffs with the latest hits, classic films, special entertainment, and cocktails, all in a historic venue erected in 1959, then revitalized in 2015.

FAST FACT

During America's drive-in heyday, fans took their love for the outdoor entertainment venues up a notch with fly-in theaters. The first fly-in, which opened in New Jersey in 1948, welcomed 500 cars and 25 private planes; the aircrafts landed at a nearby field and then taxied to the theater's back row.

LATE-NIGHT JAM SESSIONS

Rock out with musicians letting loose at these after-hours shows.

BUDGET: $ **WHEN TO GO:** Year-round   **ACTIVITY LEVEL:** Mild   **GO FOR:** Culture

Jazz is the heartbeat of Kansas City's 18th & Vine district. But to catch the best shows, you'll have to stay up late.

Every weekend, musicians far and wide flock to the district for its legendary late-night jam sessions. These raw, unscripted events are like refuges for artists once the night's gigs and concerts have wrapped. Jam sessions give musicians a chance to let go of the set list and play from the heart. Despite extending into the early hours of Sunday morning, from 1:30 a.m. to 5 a.m., jazz fans flock to these after-hours performances in droves.

Jam nights spotlight the area's renowned and budding artists and give visitors a look at the city's storied jazz past. "New Orleans is the place where jazz was born," says James McGee, Sr., a spokesperson for Kansas City's Mutual Musicians Foundation (MMF), the world's oldest continuously operating jazz house. "Kansas City is where jazz grew up."

Kansas City's jazz boom dates back to the 1920s, when the ban on alcohol presented an opportunity. While much of the country adopted strict Prohibition policies, the city's leadership followed the directions of political boss Tom Pendergast: Don't ask, don't tell, and rage on.

Loose restrictions drew revelers and artists, particularly Black musicians. "Everyone enjoyed this freedom you couldn't find in other parts of the country, especially for Black people," says McGee, noting many families at this time

OPPOSITE: **During the day, visit the American Jazz Museum to learn more of the genre's fascinating history and beginnings in Kansas City.**

PAGES 242-243: **Musicians let loose after a night of club sets for a freewheeling jam session.**

were escaping the South's Jim Crow segregation. Though the city was still subject to segregation laws, "the opportunity to live a life that was less restricted was welcome."

The loose approach helped the city's music scene blossom. During this time, the MMF skyrocketed in popularity. It saw the likes of musical icons such as Count Basie, Big Joe Turner, Charlie Parker, and Jay McShann. The house, which doubled as a local union for musicians, welcomed the first late-night jam sessions more than a century ago.

At the end of Prohibition, jazz culture dispersed beyond Kansas City. Still, musicians and fans come back and pay homage to the MMF, which is now a national historic landmark and on the list of the Kansas City Register of Historic Places.

"When you come here at 1:30 in the morning, not only are you going to hear great jazz," says McGee, "you're also going to be taken back to a time when Black musicians—this is all they had."

WHILE YOU'RE THERE

Gain a deeper appreciation for Kansas City's musical roots at the American Jazz Museum, an interactive experience with permanent and rotating films, exhibits, live music, and the on-site Blue Room, which hosts its own evening and late-night jam sessions.

DISNEY'S NIGHTLY FIREWORKS

Make magical memories at Walt Disney World's nightly fireworks shows.

BUDGET: $$ **WHEN TO GO:** Year-round   **ACTIVITY LEVEL:** Mild   **GO FOR:** Culture

I n the eyes of Walt Disney, fireworks ending a day at his California theme park were like a "kiss goodnight" to the guests. As a child, Walt was mesmerized by Fourth of July fireworks in the skies above his Missouri hometown and sought to bring that nostalgic sparkle to his own parks, first in Disneyland in the 1950s. His inaugural show, Disneyland's Fantasy in the Sky, set expectations high. Though Walt didn't live to see Walt Disney World's opening, that park continued the after-dark tradition when it opened in 1971. With today's pyrotechnic advancements, each new show debut raises the bar further.

You can enjoy Disney's nighttime spectaculars at its parks around the globe, but there's something extra magical about watching the show at one of Walt Disney World's parks in Lake Buena Vista, Florida. Magic Kingdom, EPCOT, and Disney's Hollywood Studios theme parks each run action-packed fireworks and projection shows every night of the year. The parks go particularly above and beyond for ticketed holiday season offerings, such as Mickey's Very Merry Christmas Party, with live characters, special events, light displays on the castles and buildings, narration, and music.

From Tinker Bell's flight to the colorful bursts above Cinderella Castle, Magic Kingdom's after-dark extravaganza elicits childlike wonder. Most spectators catch the show in front of the castle or along Main Street, U.S.A., where you can grab a caramel apple or Mickey Mouse ice-cream bar

WHILE YOU'RE THERE

Guests visiting Disney World's Animal Kingdom Lodge near Disney's Animal Kingdom Theme Park can partake in nighttime safaris. These VIP after-dark safaris use night vision technology to help guests admire up to 30 species of African animals.

OPPOSITE: Fireworks burst above an illuminated Cinderella Castle at Walt Disney World.

PAGES 246-247: Fireworks shows are a key part of the Disney experience throughout the various theme parks, including EPCOT.

before the music, lights, and magic commence.

With floor-to-ceiling windows looking out to Magic Kingdom, California Grill on the 15th floor of Disney's Contemporary Resort is another nighttime delight. The restaurant's high-end dining, fine wine, and decadent desserts (don't miss the crème brûlée) are set in one of the best fireworks dining experiences at Walt Disney World Resort, allowing you to enjoy the show without the crowds.

EPCOT's Luminous The Symphony of Us brings synchronized tunes, fireworks, and light displays above and on World Showcase Lagoon. You can catch the spectacle from all 11 represented nations on the Showcase's promenade loop. For dinner, snag a table at the Mexico Pavilion's La Hacienda de San Angel or the U.K.'s Rose & Crown Dining Room; book a fireworks dining package at either of these restaurants for table seating along the lagoon and standout views. Alternatively, squeeze in a ride on the Frozen Ever After attraction, then grab a drink and spot along the promenade between Mexico and Norway, which offers some of the lagoon's best panoramas.

One of the nightly shows at Disney's Hollywood Studios, Wonderful World of Animation, is a nod to the company's innovative animation, with beloved movie scenes projected across the Chinese Theatre. Fantasmic! is the bigger draw, with fireworks, lasers, projections, and live character appearances, making it a truly unique live theatrical experience in a custom-built outdoor amphitheater.

FULL-MOON VIA FERRATA

Challenge yourself by scaling rocks after dark.

BUDGET: **$$**   WHEN TO GO: **April–October**   ACTIVITY LEVEL: **Strenuous**   GO FOR: **Adventure**

If the idea of a via ferrata—scaling sheer mountains using staple-like footholds, ropes, and cables—sounds enticing, we'll up the ante: Try a via ferrata after dark.

This hair-raising adventure blends hiking and rock climbing with access to rock faces that would otherwise be unscalable for nonprofessionals. During a via ferrata adventure, adrenaline junkies climb up and across a series of fixed pieces, such as staples, cables, bridges, and ladders, for a multi-hour excursion. The sport is increasingly popular in U.S. mountain towns, but it actually started across the Atlantic.

For centuries, via ferratas helped villagers in the Alps move between mountainous towns, with a mix of iron pins, human-made footholds, and hand hooks. They were particularly useful during World War I, when Austrian and Italian soldiers clambered across rock faces in the sawtooth Dolomite mountain range during and between battles.

Today, most via ferrata courses welcome travelers during daylight for safety. But West Virginia's year-round Nelson Rocks course offers full moon via ferrata nights that really bring on the adrenaline rush.

The Nelson Rocks excursion is tucked into the secluded Potomac Highlands canyons, with climbing haven Monongahela National Forest as the backdrop. The via ferrata night route connects two rock fins with a swinging

OPPOSITE: Tether yourself to the rocks and embark on an adrenaline-fueled via ferrata adventure that begins at dusk and goes well after dark.

PAGES 250-251: The via ferrata course at Nelson Rocks includes suspended bridges, as well as ropes, hooks, and ladders.

200-foot-long (60 m) bridge, 179 steel rungs, and one mile (1.6 km) of steel cable, all more than 100 feet (30 m) above an oak-speckled canyon.

Nighttime trips run the day before, on, and after a full moon from spring through fall. Headlamps are required, but you may be surprised just how bright the full moon shines. "Due to the extreme lack of light pollution in our area, the moon's typically bright enough that we can turn headlamps off for a significant portion of the climb," says Bryan Williams of NROCKS Outdoor Adventures, which runs the excursion.

To partake, you'll first need to complete the NROCKS course or a similar via ferrata by day. Come climbing night, you'll be strapped in with a harness and led by a professional guide for the entire length of the route. The whole climb runs for anywhere from three and a half to five hours.

If rock climbing by night sounds terrifying, Williams shares some encouragement: "I tend to find that most clients find it less scary at night, possibly due to the exposure to heights being somewhat dulled by the darkness."

OTHER MARVELS

Elevate your mountain scaling with a hut-to-hut via ferrata adventure in Italy's Dolomites, the birthplace of the sport. The experience will have you clambering across the region's jagged rock fangs for multiple days, or even weeks, of heart-pumping adventure, with nights spent unwinding in cozy mountain huts.

ALCATRAZ AT NIGHT

Take a late-night tour of one of the world's most infamous penitentiaries.

BUDGET: $$ **WHEN TO GO:** Year-round **ACTIVITY LEVEL:** Mild **GO FOR:** Culture

S an Francisco Bay's Alcatraz Island earned its haunting reputation by housing some of the United States' most infamous prisoners. A day tour of the historic facility is chilling enough, but visit after hours for an extra thrill. The evening adventure embarks from San Francisco's Pier 33, known as Alcatraz Landing, just before sunset. The pink and purple sky offers a stark juxtaposition to the history of Alcatraz being shared by onboard guides. Known as the Rock, the prison opened in the mid-1800s to hold deserters and prisoners from the Civil War, the Spanish-American War, and the Boxer Rebellion. Later, it was turned into a federal penitentiary.

From the 1930s to 1960s, Alcatraz served as a maximum-security prison for the country's most dangerous and disobedient prisoners, including Al Capone and George "Machine Gun" Kelly. Though Alcatraz saw more than a dozen attempted prison escapes, including the famous jailbreak of June 1962, there are no confirmed escapees—although the fate of the fugitives from the 1962 escape remains a mystery.

Guided nighttime tours of the Rock include a walk through the cells and around prison grounds, with the chance to see places few daytime travelers get to access, such as the second floor of cells and Alcatraz Hospital. Though dozens of boats run by day, only a handful visit at dusk, so you'll enjoy this popular attraction at both its eeriest and emptiest.

OPPOSITE: Some of the United States' most infamous criminals were imprisoned at Alcatraz, and a visit after dark makes the experience even more haunting.

SYNCHRONOUS FIREFLY FESTIVAL

Find yourself mesmerized by a glittery display in Great Smoky Mountains National Park.

BUDGET: $ **WHEN TO GO:** May–June   **ACTIVITY LEVEL:** Mild   **GO FOR:** Nature

A group of lightning bugs is called a sparkle, and it only takes one night at Great Smoky Mountains National Park's synchronous fireflies event to understand why. Each spring, fireflies fill the park's oak and hickory forests with their synchronized flashes. These twinkling displays are like a visual Morse code. Lightning bugs (technically beetles) glow in tandem to locate each other for mating.

Attending the annual festival is a choice way to admire the fireflies' shine. During this one-week event, travelers head to Elkmont Campground, just outside Gatlinburg, Tennessee, to watch thousands of the beetles sparkle in patterns and naturally timed bursts. It's mesmerizing for guests; for the beetles, it's life's grand finale. The fireflies spend the majority of their one- to two-year lives in the larval stage. They chomp on forest-floor cuisine like snails and worms before "glowing up" into their adult stage, where they shimmer through the woodlands to reproduce before it's lights out.

Bioluminescence is behind the beetles' incandescence. Like jellyfish or dinoflagellates, fireflies produce their own light via their body's reaction between the chemical luciferin, luciferase enzymes, and oxygen. Their green-yellow glow is impressively efficient. Nearly 100 percent of the chemical reaction's energy is given off as light, not heat. For comparison, the

FAST FACT

Fireflies communicate via a Morse code–like system that's similar to computer language. Entomologists are working to understand this language, then replicate it to train robots to communicate via flashes, which they'll use to help locate earthquake victims or map areas in real time.

OPPOSITE: Synchronous fireflies become your nightlight while camping in Great Smoky Mountains National Park.

PAGES 256-257: Many scientists believe the light show is a firefly mating ritual.

majority of energy from an average light bulb emits as heat, not illumination.

Incandescence is only part of this phenomenon's awe power; equally impressive is the light-burst language. While female fireflies shimmer from tree branches, males flash through the sky in unison, with a series of bursts, then pure darkness, then another ripple of light. This inter-species communication is critical for finding same-species mates. Some firefly species also feast upon smaller ones and use decoy flash patterns to attract prey to the wrong place. Great Smoky Mountains National Park is home to 19 of North America's roughly 150 species of lightning bugs, including some of the only ones known to synchronously flash.

The synchronous fireflies viewing event typically starts around late May or early June, depending on firefly activity. It occurs every night for an eight-day period and runs for three to six hours at Elkmont Campground, a quiet pocket of maples and oaks located eight miles (13 km) from Gatlinburg. Upon reaching camp, you'll sit and wait for the fireflies to begin their show, which typically starts around dusk, so don't forget your lawn chair or blanket. To keep the lightning bugs safe, turn your phone off and leave flashlights in the car, or at the very least, make sure they're covered in red cellophane, which is less visible to the insects.

During the event, access to the Elkmont area is restricted after 4 p.m. Only registered campers

ABOVE: Pack a picnic and chairs: You'll watch the trees and wait for the fireflies to glow after the sun sets.

OPPOSITE: Fireflies light up Great Smoky Mountains National Park yearly around late May or early June.

and those with vehicle reservations (obtained via advanced lottery) can attend. The lottery typically opens in April and awards 100 vehicle passes per night, with each ticketed vehicle allowed up to seven passengers.

If you're unable to win a spot in the Great Smoky Mountains National Park event, don't lose hope. In Tennessee, Lamar Alexander Rocky Fork State Park offers an alternative event. Held around the same time, the state park's event is just as hard to get into, though. Only 10 vehicles (with up to six passengers each) are permitted per night. Congaree National Park in South Carolina runs an equally enchanting late-spring firefly show around the same time. At the Pennsylvania Firefly Festival in Allegheny National Forest, on the last weekend of June, 15 different firefly species shimmer through the sky. But make sure to secure your tickets in advance: Each of these events is also run via a lottery system.

NEW MEXICO, UNITED STATES

THE BAT FLIGHT

See an ancient mammalian ritual in Carlsbad Caverns National Park.

BUDGET: $ **WHEN TO GO:** May–October   **ACTIVITY LEVEL:** Mild   **GO FOR:** Wildlife

The acid-carved caves of Carlsbad Caverns National Park host one of the most surreal nighttime spectaculars: the simultaneous flight of half a million Brazilian free-tailed bats.

Just after sunset, colonies of bats whoosh from the Natural Entrance at Carlsbad Caverns all at once. They soar in a counterclockwise pattern like nocturnal acrobats on the hunt for the evening's smorgasbord of moths and beetles. It's a sensory experience for spectators seated in the park's bat-viewing amphitheater, from the mammals' chirps to their distinct, musky odor. Catch the park's free ranger-led Bat Flight Program from late May through October.

The experience begins around sunset in the Bat Amphitheater. Before the mammals emerge, park rangers provide information about the Brazilian free-tailed bats and the more than a dozen other bat species they share these caves with. Then, as dusk descends, the winged creatures spiral out of the cave and above the arena en route to dinner. In all, the experience lasts 30 minutes to an hour.

Scientists believe the mammals have zipped to and from this cave for more than 45,000 years, based on the amount of guano (bat feces) found within the cave system. But the flying mammals don't spend all of their lives here. The migratory bats follow food north each spring and south each winter. When the New Mexico weather warms, they make their way back to their roosts and give birth. During bat season, the park has around 500,000 Brazilian free-tailed bats.

OPPOSITE: Up to 500,000 Brazilian free-tailed bats live in Carlsbad Caverns National Park come summer.

PAGES 262-263: You won't enter the cave where the bats live, but you can explore parts of Carlsbad Caverns on your own or with a guide.

During the day, the mammals sleep upside down, suspended from domed ceilings deep in the cave. They're too far in to see the light change outside the cave, but the intelligent creatures know exactly when to head out for their nightly hunts. Scientists aren't sure how they tell time, but guesses include an internal clock, or that the bats notice a change in air temperature and pressure. No matter how they do it, one thing's for certain: These bats know how to find their dinner.

While visitors watch the soaring mammals from below, the park's bats gorge on around three tons (2.7 t) of insects each night. They find their chow largely by echolocation. The mammals emit a high-pitched sound (beyond the range of human hearing) that travels through the air, then bounces back to the bat once it hits an object.

Their presence is integral to the local eco-system. "Our bats' favorite meal is moths," says Michael Larson, public information officer for Carlsbad Caverns National Park, noting moths can wreak havoc on local agriculture, like cotton. "Bats save the local farmers millions of dollars in

WHILE YOU'RE THERE

Pair a bat flight with a night of ranger-led stargazing or a twilight hike, available immediately after the flight-viewing program on select summer and fall evenings. Rangers use laser pointers to spotlight the sky's best astronomical sights, while the roughly 1.5-mile (2.4 km) hikes immerse you in the dusky Chihuahuan Desert.

ABOVE: A guided lantern tour through the halls and rooms provides a unique perspective of the cave system at Carlsbad Caverns.

OPPOSITE: Take in the wondrous and towering cave formation—with only a headlamp illuminating your way.

pesticide applications. They are key players in balancing and controlling insect populations."

Yet, like many of their relatives, Carlsbad Caverns' bats face serious threats. White-nose syndrome, a deadly fungus, has killed millions of bats in 40 states over the past two decades. It's largely spread through bat-to-bat contact, but humans can accidentally transport the fungus via shoes, clothes, and equipment. That's why Carlsbad Cavern officials ask visitors to never enter a cave wearing gear worn in another cave without cleaning it first.

For prime bat viewing, visit in August and September. These months see the highest numbers of bats, as the young Brazilian free-tailed pups become old enough to fly and hunt on their own. Before you enter the amphitheater, take note: Electronics are forbidden because flashes and noise can change the animals' behavior.

BLACK-WATER DIVING

Immerse yourself in the world's largest migration.

BUDGET: $$ **WHEN TO GO:** March–June **ACTIVITY LEVEL:** Intermediate **GO FOR:** Wildlife

Wildlife lovers travel far and wide to admire Earth's great migrations, from the 1.5 million wildebeest crossing the Mara River in East Africa to the monarch butterflies fluttering from Canada to Mexico. Yet the world's largest migration occurs in the ocean, and like clockwork, it takes place every night.

Once night falls, around 11 billion tons (10 billion t) of sea creatures rocket from what's known as the ocean's dim twilight zone, found between 650 to 3,280 feet (200 to 1,000 m) deep, up toward the surface, where they feed and then descend just before sunrise. The migratory movement is the equivalent of humans running a six-mile (9.6 km) race at twice the speed of an Olympic marathoner and doing so every day. The cloud of sea critters is also so dense it shows up as a false bottom on echo sounders (tools that determine seabed depth).

Scuba diving is your ticket to the hypnotic happening, and for that, Palm Beach on Florida's Atlantic coast provides an ideal base camp. The Gulf Stream current offers the right mix of water temperature and nutrient flow to foster the after-dark marvel, known as the diel vertical migration. The stream travels closer to the Palm Beach shores than virtually anywhere else on Florida's coasts, and local dive shops, such as Pura Vida Divers, have made the most of it.

OPPOSITE: While watching micro-life migrate from the bottom of the ocean, you'll also see larger species like moon jellyfish.

PAGES 268-269: A rare appearance—a whale shark swims in the waters just off the coast of Palm Beach, Florida.

To see these migrators—mostly zooplankton like small fish, jellies, and shrimp, or even rare species like the lantern fish—scuba outfitters run black-water drift dives that illuminate the evening activity with subtle dive lights. "It's like no other night dive you'll experience," says Andrea Whitaker, a guide with South Florida–based Pura Vida Divers.

Your night starts with a 45-minute sunset cruise offshore to reach a stretch of ocean deep enough for the migration to take place. Once you're in the water, you'll drift with the current and stay shallow—no more than 50 feet (15 m) deep. Unlike most dives, this trip is less about deep descents to see marine species. Instead, all that life comes up and whirs, flips, and spins past you—from sparkling bioluminescent comb jellies to translucent squid that look straight out of a science fiction film. The surrounding water is jet-black, save your dive lights and the glowing black-water rig— a surface float ball with an illuminated 40-foot (12 m) line and reference point.

In addition to the miniature migrators, as well as larger lantern fish and squid, you may spot other stunners, such as seahorses, sharks, octopus, or sea turtles. During summer's sea turtle nesting season, you could even spot hatchlings hiding among sargassum seaweed at the surface.

The creatures that take part in this nightly migration do more than just dazzle divers; they play an integral role in carbon sequestration. The migrators ingest carbon at the ocean's

surface, then release it via waste in the deep water, where it's stored in the seafloor—instead of our atmosphere—for decades, and even centuries.

You'll need at least a Professional Association of Diving Instructors (PADI) advanced open water or night diver certification to partake in these dives. Or, with Pura Vida, divers can get the Blackwater Drift Diver Specialty certification. Trips run year-round, but late spring through early summer, when the ocean is calmest, provide the best experience. Other destinations making a splash with black-water diving include Hawaii, the Philippines, and Palau.

Craving out-of-this-world fun? Head about two hours north of Palm Beach to Florida's Space Coast. Its main attraction, the Kennedy Space Center, impresses with astronomical history, astronaut encounters, the fascinating Hubble Space Telescope Theater, and the chance to watch a live rocket launch.

ABOVE: Just a short drive from Palm Beach, you can watch a space shuttle launch from the Kennedy Space Center.

OPPOSITE: As part of the nightly migration, a flying fish makes its way back to the depths of the ocean.

RED ROCKS AMPHITHEATRE

Dance the night away at crag-flanked concerts in this Colorado haunt.

BUDGET: $$ **WHEN TO GO:** April–November **ACTIVITY LEVEL:** Mild **GO FOR:** Culture

J am out beneath the starry skies and layered sandstone with a concert at Red Rocks Amphitheatre. This legendary Colorado music venue, nestled in the foothills of the Rocky Mountains about 30 minutes southwest of Denver, is part natural wonder, part acoustic marvel.

Music travels up from the deep stage, then bounces off the 300-foot-tall (90 m) monolithic walls. These rocky bookends, each nearly as tall as London's Big Ben, retain sound within the 9,500-person amphitheater. The result: a jam-packed night with some of the best musical acts in the world.

The venue officially opened in June 1941 with a performance from the New York Metropolitan Opera. The past few decades have welcomed world-renowned acts to the Red Rocks stage, including Louis Armstrong, Ray Charles, B. B. King, Jimi Hendrix, the Rolling Stones, and even the Beatles, who put on one of the venue's most iconic shows in August 1964. More recent performers include the Chainsmokers, Incubus, and the Black Keys.

Concerts, film screenings, and comedy nights bring this national historic landmark to life come dusk, with laser and light displays that paint the surrounding stone, while Denver's twinkling skyline shines bright on the horizon. Shows run in the evenings from spring through fall. During daytime visits, enjoy a self-guided venue tour or peruse past musical acts in the amphitheater's Colorado Music Hall of Fame.

OPPOSITE: Beloved musicians from Joni Mitchell to Dave Matthews have performed on stage at Red Rocks.

SLEEP AT PHANTOM RANCH

Land one of America's most coveted reservations at Grand Canyon National Park.

BUDGET: $$-$$$ **WHEN TO GO:** March–May or September–November
ACTIVITY LEVEL: Strenuous **GO FOR:** Adventure

The Grand Canyon's allure entices nature enthusiasts with sprawling striated canyons and geologic marvels. Millions visit annually for a day trip or a hike halfway to the canyon's floor. But a lucky few—less than one percent of all Grand Canyon visitors—get to spend the night at Phantom Ranch, the only lodging beneath the canyon rim.

Phantom Ranch, a sprinkling of spartan dormitories and cabins on the canyon floor, has occupied the rocky base for more than a century. Erecting accommodations at the bottom of this world wonder was no easy feat. It took two years of heavy labor and mules toting building supplies down the canyon's steep terrain to make it happen. The design, the brainchild of architect Mary Jane Colter, called for locally sourced stone and wood to ensure the lodge seamlessly blends with its desert surrounds.

These days, Phantom Ranch is a place of legend for national park travelers—and one of the hardest-to-nab hotel reservations in the United States. In fact, the ranch, part of the National Trust for Historic Preservation's Historic Hotels of America list, is so popular it requires a lottery that almost always books up more than a year out. Those who don't win the lottery can also apply for a permit to camp at Bright Angel Campground on the canyon floor. It may not be the coveted ranch reservation, but Bright Angel campers do have access to the hearty home-cooked Phantom Ranch meals (including a

FAST FACT

Learn about the Hualapai tribe, one of the 11 Indigenous communities associated with the park, via Grand Canyon West. Here, you can enjoy live music from the Hualapai Bird Singers before heading to the Grand Canyon Skywalk, a glass bridge jutting out over the canyon.

OPPOSITE: On a Colorado River rafting trip, you'll make camp—and enjoy a night by a bonfire—on the Grand Canyon's floor along the river's shores.

PAGES 276-277: Phantom Ranch, designed by Mary Colter, was completed in 1922.

signature beef stew and vegetarian chili), not to mention its nearby marvels: colorful canyon walls, the Colorado River, and Bright Angel Creek.

There are three ways to reach Phantom Ranch: by mule, hiking, or rafting the Colorado River. Mule trips and river rides can be booked with local adventure outfitters. Hiking is the most common transit mode; jaunts typically start from the canyon's South Rim, the site of the main visitors center.

Hit the Bright Angel Trail for a nearly 10-mile (16 km) hike down to the floor; it takes roughly four to six hours. Another option, the South Kaibab Trail, is a 7.5-mile (12 km) trek of between four and six hours. As you descend on either route, you'll notice the canyon surroundings shift from copper streaks to green cacti and the distant Colorado River. A final progress marker, the suspension bridge over the river, means your overnight is within reach.

A word of warning: The downhill hike in is the easy part. Allot more time on the tail end of your trip as you climb nearly 5,000 vertical feet (1,520 m) of switchbacks up and out to the South Rim. (Experts say only travelers with the highest fitness level can do an out-and-back canyon floor climb in one day.)

If you think reaching your canyon floor abode is magical, just wait until the sun sets. The Grand Canyon is a DarkSky International–certified Dark Sky Park. That means you can see the cosmos—the same nightscapes Indigenous people have been watching here for millennia—while enjoying a rare national park view that's well worth every bead of sweat.

ALL ABOARD THE STAR TRAIN

Ride a historic railway deep into the starlit Great Basin Desert.

BUDGET: $ **WHEN TO GO:** May–September **ACTIVITY LEVEL:** Mild **GO FOR:** Stargazing

I n the early 1900s, the Nevada Northern Railway put the remote town Ely on the copper mining map. More than a century later, the railway's historic locomotives still tote riders into Nevada's piñon- and juniper-dotted Steptoe Valley—although visitors now come seeking a different sparkly prize: clear, bedazzled nightscapes. They'll find this rare bounty aboard the special-edition Star Train, which runs deep into the Great Basin Desert.

Up to 80 percent of Americans can't see the Milky Way due to light pollution. The same can't be said for those at the far-flung Great Basin, which covers much of Nevada. This 190,000-square-mile (492,000 km²) high-desert patchwork of sagebrush grasslands, rolling mountains, and broad valleys, boasts some of the country's darkest nightscapes. The Nevada Northern Railway, now a national historic landmark in Ely, roughly four hours north of Las Vegas by car, makes the most of the celestial entertainment via the Star Train, which departs around sunset on select Fridays between May and September.

As the desert transitions from honey-hued golden hour to coal black night, onboard rangers from nearby Great Basin National Park and railway staff share tidbits about the night sky attractions that await. Once you've reached your final destination—a private Great Basin viewing pad with high-powered telescopes—rangers narrate the universe's marvels, from Saturn's iridescent rings to any stargazer's beloved treasure, the glowing Milky Way.

OPPOSITE: **The Milky Way hovers above the mountains in Nevada's Great Basin National Park, easily seen from the Star Tram.**

MANTA RAY SNORKELING

Catch the dance of the mantas on an after-dark swim.

BUDGET: $$ **WHEN TO GO:** April–September   **ACTIVITY LEVEL:** Intermediate   **GO FOR:** Wildlife

Fasten your snorkel and mask for one of Hawaii's most inspiring twilight happenings: the dance of the manta rays. Beneath the glow of the moon, snorkelers float along the Kona coast off the island of Hawaii, also known as the Big Island, as creatures loop the loop and feed below. "It's like an underwater ballet," says Iko Balanga, a native Hawaiian who introduced a fresh, sustainable method of manta snorkeling via outfitter Anelakai Adventures: paddle-powered tours instead of motorized.

Large groups of resident mantas, known as squadrons, have turned the Kona coast into a night snorkeling oasis. Travelers trot the globe to see these colossal creatures, which can weigh more than 4,000 pounds (1,815 kg) with a roughly 20-foot (6 m) wingspan. You can admire them all day, but nights are especially entrancing. Outfitters install boat-bottom lightboards to attract the rays' favorite snack, plankton, which in turn draw the gentle giants to come feed.

Anelakai Adventures uses handmade double-hull *va'a* canoes, the vessels ancient Polynesians used to navigate the Pacific millennia ago. You'll paddle beneath the constellations, then don snorkel gear and ankle floats to bob at the surface as the graceful goliaths dance below. Local guides have logged more than 320 individual manta rays near Kona. "Each one

FAST FACT

Manta rays make self-care a priority with regular stops at "cleaning stations," the stretches of a coral reef where small fish and crustaceans eat bacteria and parasites off the rays' bodies. You can snorkel or dive along these manta spas off the Kona coast and along Maui's Olowalu reef.

OPPOSITE: More than 300 manta rays have been identified off Hawaii's Kona coast.

PAGES 282-283: Under-boat lighting illuminates the manta rays' food source, drawing them to the area where divers and snorkelers can watch in delight.

of their bellies has a different marking, like a fingerprint; it's how you can tell who is who," says Balanga.

Calm surface floating is crucial to keep the mantas protected; any sudden movement could spook them. That's why free diving is not allowed, nor is touching the rays. Oils from your skin can damage their protective mucus coating, making them vulnerable to infection.

Instead of handling the rays, Balanga tells his guests to interact with them through gentle noises. "We ask everyone to sing, hum, or even talk to the mantas because they love people," he says, noting they're highly intelligent.

They're also central to Hawaiian culture. The Hawaiian word for manta ray is *hāhālua; hā* means "breath of life," and *lua* is the word for two. "When Hawaiians first saw them and their big mouths, they thought the rays would take two giant breaths, then stay underwater forever," says Balanga. Many Hawaiians see the manta as their *aumakua,* or spirit animal.

Native culture and history lessons are interwoven into Balanga's nighttime snorkel tours. You can enjoy the trip year-round, but choppier winter months do bring more weather-based cancellations. Va'a canoes take six guests each outing, with two trips a night. Balanga's team welcomes nonswimmers, including young kids and those with mobility issues, to stay on board and watch the manta magic from above.

HAWAI'I VOLCANOES NATIONAL PARK

Watch the lava flow on the Big Island.

BUDGET: $ **WHEN TO GO:** Year-round   **ACTIVITY LEVEL:** Intermediate   **GO FOR:** Nature

Seeing flame-orange lava ooze from a caldera is like snagging a glimpse of inner Earth. Few places offer this kind of magma observation like Hawai'i Volcanoes National Park, home to two of the world's most active volcanoes: Mauna Loa and Kilauea. To catch that fiery magma glow, visiting after nightfall is best.

The 523-square-mile (1,354 km²) park on the island of Hawaii, also known as the Big Island, stays open 24 hours a day, with trails and observation spots customized for eruptions. "Part of our mission is to provide safe access to active volcanism," says Jessica Ferracane, spokesperson for the national park, noting access varies based on volcanic activity.

Mauna Loa and Kilauea aren't always erupting—and when they do erupt, they don't always spurt lava in the same fashion. That means it's hard to plan a Hawai'i Volcanoes National Park experience too far in advance. It largely depends on the eruption du jour (or lack thereof). Sometimes, a route like the 11-mile (17.7 km) Crater Rim Trail provides the best lava overlooks. Other nights, the park hosts a series of vantage points to admire a massive lava lake in Halemaumau, the Kilauea summit crater. Third-party operators also run after-dark boat tours to catch the spectacle as lava spills into the ocean—actively expanding the Big Island as the lava cools to rock.

"I don't know of any other national park in the whole park system where

WHERE TO STAY

Sleep on the edge of the Kilauea caldera at Volcano House, the only hotel within the national park. Just a short walk from the Kilauea Visitor Center, it has welcomed esteemed guests such as Mark Twain, Amelia Earhart, and John F. Kennedy over more than a century in business.

OPPOSITE: Lava from the Kilauea volcano spills into the ocean, setting off clouds of steam as it cools into lava rock, essentially expanding the island.

PAGES 286-287: The Halemaumau crater is Kilauea's most active vent, visible from the Crater Rim Trail in the park.

the landscape changes almost on a daily basis," says Ferracane. This goes for not just the volcano viewing, but also for the terrain itself. Volcanic activity has led to temporary closures of trails, areas, or even the entire park. The best bet to avoid trip mishaps and to keep an eye on potential eruptions? Visit the National Park Service website, or call the visitors center before you arrive.

If you're lucky enough to visit during an eruption, Ferracane recommends planning your trip for predawn. "My favorite time is 4 a.m. You can see the lava glow, then the sun comes up and lightens all the caldera walls."

After-dark visits to Hawai'i Volcanoes National Park do require some safety essentials. Bring a flashlight or headlamp and wear sturdy closed-toe shoes. If you're visiting during an eruption, wear long pants and a long-sleeve shirt to protect your body.

Even during non-eruption times, these national park nights can wow with hikes through lava tubes, permit-required backcountry camping, a blanket of stars, and the Milky Way ribbon.

Rangers also lead periodic stargazing tours through the park, and another can't-beat spot for skygazing and sunrise is nearby Mauna Kea, a dormant and snowcapped shield volcano that towers 13,796 feet (4,205 m) above sea level. Its summit is home to the Kama'āina Observatory. Visits to Mauna Kea's summit are permitted, but remember that Mauna Kea and other volcanoes are sacred places to Hawaii Natives as representations of Pele, the fire goddess.

PUERTO RICO, UNITED STATES

BIOLUMINESCENT BAY PADDLING

See the water streak electric blue with every stroke of your oar in this bioluminescent bay.

BUDGET: $$ **WHEN TO GO:** December–April   **ACTIVITY LEVEL:** Intermediate   **GO FOR:** Nature

Ethereal Mosquito Bay is proof that magic exists on planet Earth. The waters along this palm-fringed sliver of the island of Vieques in Puerto Rico explode with shimmering teal pinpricks by night. The glow's source: microscopic, one-celled dinoflagellates known as *Pyrodinium bahamense*.

A clear-bottom kayak is your best perch to see the bioluminescence in action. "It's like you're traveling through space at hyper speed," says Hailey Metz of Vieques outfitter Black Beard Sports, which offers these twilight paddles.

The bioluminescent creatures live throughout the ocean, but only five ecosystems in the world have high enough concentrations to officially have the title of bioluminescent bay. In 2006, Guinness World Records certified Puerto Rico's Mosquito Bay as the world's brightest "bioluminescent bay," with each gallon (3.8 L) of water containing up to 700,000 dinoflagellates.

The bay's bright blue bounty stems from its natural makeup. Its narrow entrance to the sea keeps the dinoflagellates from escaping. Crystal clear water helps the sunlight-reliant organisms thrive, while the dark, unpolluted skies make the neon bursts even brighter to surface-level admirers.

The glow is both dazzling and dynamic. Dinoflagellates produce light whenever a force, such as a kayak paddle or hand stroke, disrupts them. Scientists believe the organisms use their sparkle to fend off predators. The light

WHERE TO STAY

Catching Mosquito Bay's bioluminescence requires an overnight on Vieques. For that, try sleek Hix Island House, a sustainable hotel on a 13-acre (5 ha) natural refuge teeming with butterflies and birds.

OPPOSITE: Tiny actions—like a fish jumping to the paddle of an oar—set off the bioluminescent reaction in the bay.

PAGES 290-291: See the water glow from the shoreline as ripples and animal movement incite the bioluminescence.

burst startles hunters, curbing the number of plankton they can consume. Their hues also serve as a dinner bell for fish higher up the food chain, turning the planktons' predators into prey. It's a proven defense strategy, and one these tiny creatures have honed over their more than 400 million years on the planet.

Vieques Island, accessible via a roughly 45-minute boat ride from the Ceiba port on mainland Puerto Rico, delights by day with black sand shores, free-roaming horses, and the ecologically diverse Vieques National Wildlife Refuge. Come sunset, particularly on dark, new-moon nights, the enchantment begins.

Guided kayak trips start with a talk about the phenomenon and the red mangrove ecosystem that supports it. Then you'll glide along the bay for around an hour, with the stars flickering overhead and navy water sparkling beneath your vessel.

The bay shines year-round, but is at its best during Puerto Rico's dry season, from December to April; too much rainfall can dilute the effect. Environmental factors also play a role in the display's vibrancy. After Hurricane Maria in 2017, Mosquito Bay's lights temporarily dimmed, as heavy wind and rain destroyed the mangroves that support these dinoflagellates. Populations have since rebounded, and some scientists say the plankton quantities are now higher than they were pre-hurricane.

To help keep them that way, Metz asks guests to skip the bug spray: "Chemicals packed into these bug sprays are toxic to the dinoflagellates."

COSTA RICA

NOCTURNAL JUNGLE HIKE

Enjoy a community conservation success story.

BUDGET: **$$**   WHEN TO GO: **Year-round**   ACTIVITY LEVEL: **Intermediate**   GO FOR: **Nature**

Symphonies of *ribbits* and cricket calls ricochet through Costa Rica's dusk-blanketed rainforest. As darkness floods the woodlands, a faint Baird's tapir whistle may join the chorus. Though the roughly 500-pound (225 kg) tapir is Costa Rica's largest mammal, it's also one of the most challenging to spot. It's nocturnal, shy, and endangered, with poaching and habitat loss largely to blame.

Yet Tapir Valley Nature Reserve, a revitalization and ecotourism project in the rainforest of northern Costa Rica, is giving this megafauna a leg up. Night hikes are an integral part of the equation.

The 220-acre (90 ha) reserve, 130 miles (210 km) northwest of capital city San José, is among the country's best tapir-sighting areas. It's also home to around 430 bird species, 40 amphibian species, and 14 types of bats.

Night hikes to admire this biodiversity begin around 5:30 p.m. You'll start at an observation deck to watch day transition to night. "Crickets, frogs, owls—everything is a new sound," says Tapir Valley Nature Reserve co-owner Donald Varela Soto. Guests enjoy homemade empanadas from Soto's mother as sunset's last sprays of orange and blush leave the sky. Then it's time to fasten your headlamp and make your way into the pitch-black forest.

Every night trip is different in this amalgam of wetland, rainforest, secondary jungle, and grassland. You could spot frogs, bats, owls, spiders, snakes, or

FAST FACT

In 2022, Tapir Valley Nature Reserve co-owner Donald Varela Soto noticed a sound he'd never heard before. That auditory clue led to the discovery of a new species, the Tapir Valley tree frog. The tiny green frog can only be found in the Tapir Valley Nature Reserve wetlands.

OPPOSITE: Listen to the jungle come alive with sounds of wildlife, including the whistle of the elusive tapir.

PAGES 294-295: Take in the jungle views at dusk from the open-air observation points in Tapir Valley Nature Reserve.

sleeping birds. On lucky nights, your trip may include a tapir. It's by no means guaranteed, yet successful community-led conservation efforts have made the sighting more likely.

Two decades ago, Soto and a team of conservationists from the adjacent Bijagua community purchased this swath of land in hopes they could revitalize and protect the local fauna, as the valley had become a hot spot for tapir poaching. In 1999, a study declared the mammals extinct in this region. Ecotourism helped bring them back.

Building and maintaining trails, establishing camera traps, and running tours ensures a consistent presence here—one that discourages poachers. Tourism revenue also supports the Bijagua community, who are employed as local guides and trail maintainers among other roles, which helps deter residents from poaching in the first place. "The story basically goes from a community where tapirs were gone to a point where the community symbol is now the tapir," says Costa Rican biologist Esteban Brenes-Mora, noting the mammal's symbol is etched into the town's logo.

Nocturnal hikes center on spotting and listening to wildlife, but guides also use the time to spotlight the threats facing Costa Rica's ecosystems and the potential solutions. Tapir Valley is an example of what happens when you remove cows and start letting nature take over," says Brenes-Mora, noting cattle ranching is a lead cause of deforestation. "You can make a living out of conserving and protecting your land."

DÍA DE LOS MUERTOS

Get in the spirit with the Day of the Dead celebration.

BUDGET: $–$$ **WHEN TO GO:** November 1–2   **ACTIVITY LEVEL:** Mild   **GO FOR:** Culture

Día de los Muertos is one of the most important nights in Mexico. The holiday, inscribed to the UNESCO Intangible Cultural Heritage of Humanity list in 2008, is a time to honor and celebrate those who have passed. "We believe this is a day to remember the good things, and the good moments," says Ubish Yaren, owner of Mexico City–based outfitter Mexico Underground.

Events tied to this timeless holiday run the gamut. You can join festivals, enjoy live music, watch Día de los Muertos parades (known as *muerteadas*), and admire light shows or fireworks late into the night. But the most traditional Día de los Muertos evenings tend to be more muted, says Yaren. Mexicans bring candles, flowers, and food to the graves of their deceased loved ones; sometimes mariachis join too.

The holiday, which typically runs from November 1 to 2, blends Indigenous culture and New Age religion. Indigenous Mexican communities long honored the dead with practices that largely stemmed from the Aztec who believed in the afterlife. When the Spanish invaded Mexico in the 1500s, their early November Catholic All Souls' Day traditions fused with Indigenous celebrations, ultimately meshing the two traditions. This hybrid is what you'll see celebrated across the country today.

You can partake in Día de los Muertos throughout Mexico, but a handful

FAST FACT

Mexico City's Great Day of the Dead parade only started in 2016. A scene from the James Bond film *Spectre* inspired the festival, which has quickly become one of the country's largest events. It features floats, traveling altars, and the holiday's famous skulls, known as *calaveras*.

OPPOSITE: During Día de los Muertos, communities pay tribute to the dead with ornate displays.

PAGES 298-299: Celebrators paint their faces with traditional *calavera* (skull) designs, a symbol of connection to the dead.

of places go all out with old and new traditions. Experience it on your own or hire a local guide for a deeper understanding of the holiday's past and present.

San Agustín Etla in Oaxaca runs raucous after-dark Día de los Muertos parties featuring battle-of-the-bands-style live music performances. And a muerteada, featuring costumed dancers, makes its way through the streets of San Agustín Etla after dark on November 1.

In Xochimilco, a UNESCO World Heritage site just outside Mexico City, boats fill the canals with candlelight on a procession to the San Gregorio Atlapulco cemetery. Travelers can join the twinkling convoy via a *trajinera* (traditional Mexican boat) tour.

Janitzio is a small island in Lake Pátzcuaro in western Mexico's Michoacán. Here the Purépecha community hosts traditional Día de los Muertos events like Animecha Kejtsïtakua (translated to the Night of the Dead), where fisherman take to the lake in wooden candlelit canoes while families march toward the local graveyard with torches, lights, and packed feasts. The cemetery bell, rung to awaken the souls, is the evening's soundtrack.

Even beyond these hot spots, you can experience Día de los Muertos throughout the country. Yaren says local gatherings in neighborhoods, towns, and villages are less crowded and more authentic than some of the boisterous parties that now fill the city streets. His tip for a true experience: "Look for the local graveyard."

GUATEMALA

GO OWLING

Perk your ears for a hoot of a time birding at night.

BUDGET: $–$$ **WHEN TO GO:** Year-round **ACTIVITY LEVEL:** Intermediate **GO FOR:** Nature

A hoot is the first sign an owl might be close. Cup your hand to your ear and you just may decipher its direction. Whether or not you actually spot the bird is up to fate, but that's the gamble during a night of owling. It's like birding, but after dark, and avian oasis Guatemala is one of the best places to give it a go.

Birders flock to Guatemala for its more than 700 bird species, from the Yucatán flycatcher to the resplendent quetzal, the national bird. It's also an important migratory corridor for avian creatures. The northern Guatemala Maya Biosphere Reserve, the largest tropical rainforest north of the Amazon, provides a protected stopover.

Guatemala's owl populations are equally impressive. The country has at least 20 owl species, plus other nocturnal birds like nighthawks and potoos. Los Tarrales Natural Reserve, located near Guatemala's Atitlán Volcano, is an ideal spot for owling excursions. More than 350 types of birds have been recorded here, and nearly a dozen owl species make that list. The reserve lodge has 11 rooms with multiple daily and nightly excursions, including nocturnal tours to see owls, bats, kinkajous, and—if you're lucky—the elusive puma.

Another avian hot spot is Guatemala's Tikal National Park, located within the 142,330-acre (57,600 ha) Maya Biosphere Reserve, a UNESCO World Heritage site. Nocturnal sightings around this maze of Maya ruins include the ferruginous pygmy owl, the mottled owl, and the barn owl. Avid birders should also visit during the day, when they'll have the chance to spot more than 400 species.

OPPOSITE: Illuminated, the Maya Temple of the Great Jaguar shines at Guatemala's Tikal National Park.

THE TURTLE ARRIBADA

See hundreds—maybe even thousands—of nesting sea turtles.

BUDGET: $$ **WHEN TO GO:** July-November **ACTIVITY LEVEL:** Intermediate **GO FOR:** Wildlife

S leep is impossible when an *arribada* is on the horizon. The arribada, or arrival, is a simultaneous nighttime nesting event that brings hundreds to thousands of sea turtles ashore. The females gather in the shallow waters, then crawl onto the moonlit beach in unison. Once on dry land, each reptile lays around 100 eggs, then furiously kicks sand to disguise the nest before inching back to sea.

Only two species are known to nest en masse like this, Kemp's ridley and olive ridley sea turtles, and they do so on just a handful of beaches from Central America to India. Panama has two arribada spots, both in its southern Tonosí District: Playa La Marinera and Isla Cañas. The latter, a small village of some 700 people on the country's Pacific side, is the site of a successful conservation project. Guided arribada night tours are integral to the initiative.

An arribada is one of the most astonishing wildlife scenes you can witness. With so many turtles nesting at once, "it's almost impossible to walk around the beach," says Daniel Pérez of Isla Cañas' agro-ecotourism group, which co-leads the sea turtle conservation program.

For millennia, people around the world have hunted turtles and their eggs for consumption. Harvesting, paired with bycatch from fishing gear and habitat degradation, have led to plummeting sea turtle populations globally. The mass breeding technique of the Kemp's ridley and olive ridley

OTHER MARVELS

Panama is one of only three carbon-negative countries in the world— a feat achieved largely through its mangroves, which hold more than 50 million tons (45 million t) of carbon.
The boat- and paddle-friendly Isla Cañas mangrove trail inspires locals who once harvested these natural resources to now safeguard them.

OPPOSITE: Thousands of olive ridley sea turtles gather ashore to nest and lay their eggs.

PAGES 304-305: Volunteers help count eggs to track turtle population levels and protect their nests.

species makes them particularly easy targets.

Increasingly, numerous countries have enacted national bans on killing turtles or collecting their eggs, which has gradually yielded conservation wins for the creatures. One such example of conservation success is the Isla Cañas community-based sea turtle initiative.

The arribada occurs almost exclusively on a 1.2-mile (2 km) strip of protected beach, the Isla Cañas Wildlife Refuge. Volunteers move any eggs laid outside of this area to a protected nursery within the refuge to increase hatchling survival odds. When the arribada begins, eco-police patrol the shore. Meanwhile, licensed guides bring travelers out to watch the spectacle.

These days, the community sees a live turtle as more valuable than a harvested one, says Pérez, noting ecotourism revenue uplifts locally owned culinary, transportation, guiding, and lodging businesses. Tourism is an even more viable option for the village following the country's rollout of the SOSTUR network, a platform that directly links travelers with responsible and authentic tourism experiences in Panama's Indigenous and rural communities, including Isla Cañas.

Panama's arribada occurs roughly once a month between July and November, over one to two days. It's tricky to predict the event, although the arrivals tend to happen about 30 to 35 days apart.

Roughly 45 days after nesting, hatchlings start their journeys from eggshell to sea. Guided tours run to witness both enthralling events.

NIGHT ZIP LINES

Soar beneath the stars.

BUDGET: $-$$ **WHEN TO GO:** March–November   **ACTIVITY LEVEL:** Strenuous   **GO FOR:** Adventure

Zip-lining by day promises heart-pumping fun, but speeding from tree to tree beneath the full moon's pale glow or a sky splashed with stars? That's some next-level adrenaline. You can snag your dose of it with after-hours zip lines all across the United States.

In southeastern Ohio, Hocking Hills Canopy Tours leads intrepid guests on moonshine zips during full-moon nights from June to October. The course's half dozen lines race by the Hocking Hills region's signature gorge landscapes: sandstone cliffs, recessed caverns, and a patchwork of firefly-bejeweled pines. During one of the course's highlights, adventurers even zip by a waterfall and into a cave. This two-hour moonlit trip is available roughly an hour from Columbus.

In Austin, Texas, you'll find another canopy gem: Lake Travis Zipline Adventures, one of the country's longest and fastest zip-line courses. Its full moon ride takes three hours to complete and includes five zips and a jaw-dropping grand finale: leaping down 20 stories to zip 2,800 feet (853 m) across Lake Travis. The moonlight, glow sticks, and a headlamp work in tandem to illuminate your path. This outing runs on full-moon nights from March to November; weekly starlit night tours are also available every Saturday.

For a surreal peek at Sin City, book an after-dark trip on SlotZilla, a towering zip line that resembles a larger-than-life slot machine in Las Vegas,

OPPOSITE: **Fly high and fast across a zip line with Sky Valley Zip Tours' Night Flight in North Carolina.**

PAGES 308-309: **For a high-stakes thrill, consider a zip line over Fremont Street in the Old Vegas area of Las Vegas, Nevada.**

Nevada. The route flies over downtown Fremont Street, a historic Old Vegas area renowned for its neon signs and shimmering marquees. SlotZilla runs two course options: The Zip-Zilla departs from a seven-story platform and travels for two blocks, and the Super-Hero Zoom, a route that starts 114 feet (35 m) off the ground and speeds 40 miles (64 km) an hour down five blocks of Fremont Street, ends at the Golden Gate Hotel & Casino.

Over in North Carolina's rippling Blue Ridge Mountains, night owls can hitch a ride on the Sky Valley Zip Tours moonlit course. This pathway spans five stretches of the facility's canopy tour, including a heart-pumping 1,600-foot (490 m) zip line across a sea of maples and hemlocks, with a headlamp and the glittery cosmos lighting your way. End the adrenaline-packed night with a cliff jump before catching an ATV ride back to your car. Night flights run on weekends, with the excursion launching after sunset.

OTHER MARVELS

Zip lines do more than fuel adrenaline. For centuries, people in the world's most rugged, mountainous regions—such as the Himalaya—built zip lines rather than bridges to travel and transfer goods. You can experience this traditional mountain transit at ZipFlyer Nepal, one of the world's steepest zip lines. It drops nearly 2,000 feet (610 m) and soars at more than 60 miles (96 km) an hour. For safety, night zips are not available here.

PART FIVE

OCEANIA

The Milky Way brightens the night sky
over the Karlu Karlu / Devils Marbles
Conservation Reserve in Australia's
Northern Territory (page 312).

OUTBACK ASTRONOMY

Admire pristine nightscapes in Australia's red desert.

BUDGET: $–$$$$ **WHEN TO GO:** Year-round   **ACTIVITY LEVEL:** Mild   **GO FOR:** Stargazing

For at least 60,000 years, the Aboriginal and Torres Strait Islander communities—some of the world's first astronomers—used planets, constellations, and dark space to track food sources and pass down generational knowledge. Many have retained this deep-sky connection and now share it with travelers via astrotourism, particularly in Australia's rugged and remote outback.

Light pollution plagues destinations around the world; only a sliver of the human population can see the Milky Way from their home. That's not the case in the wild outback. This dry expanse covers more than 70 percent of the continent, including much of the Northern Territory. The erosion-carved landscapes seesaw between rusty red desert and deep gorges, with the outback's best known feature, Uluru–Kata Tjuta National Park, a UNESCO World Heritage site that's reachable via desert gateway town Alice Springs in the Northern Territory.

The site earned UNESCO status for its geological marvels, natural importance and beauty, and sacredness to the Anangu people—one of the world's oldest living cultures and the traditional inhabitants of this parkland.

You can admire polka-dotted night skies from any outback perch, but a night that intertwines Indigenous astronomy with deep space gazing promises the ultimate awe and enrichment.

OTHER MARVELS

Wycliffe Well, around 200 miles (320 km) north of Alice Springs, is considered the UFO capital of Australia. Visitors have reported seeing UFOs here since World War II, with so many unexplained occurrences the Royal Australian Air Force has even come out to investigate reports.

OPPOSITE: With virtually no light pollution, the skies above Uluru provide phenomenal views of the cosmos.

PAGES 314–315: Along with stars, you'll find 30,000-year-old rock art throughout Uluru–Kata Tjuta National Park.

Earth Sanctuary, a sustainable tourist and education venue outside Alice Springs, runs a host of night sky programming. Astronomer-led events spotlight supergiants, constellations, and planets, with night sky knowledge often shared by Anangu people. For an around-the-clock night of space scouting, book an overnight stargazing package. This includes sky-viewing and fireside discussions about the universe while camping on the Earth Sanctuary grounds.

The national park's sacred 1,142-foot-tall (348 m) Uluru monolith stands grand above the tawny desert. When twilight's darkness decks the Uluru skies with stars and planets, the scene can feel transcendent. Light pollution is virtually nonexistent here, with the closest major town, Alice Springs, hours away. Ayers Rock Resort, located near Uluru–Kata Tjuta National Park, is the perfect home base for daytime adventures like hiking and culinary workshops, with a host of after-hours events that center on the getaways' natural resource: unobstructed nightscapes. The resort's most popular evening tour, the outdoor Sounds of Silence dinner, includes a mix of culture, cuisine, and astronomy. Guests learn about native ingredients from the chef on a dune-top dining table, then meet with Ayers Rock Resort's resident astronomer to navigate the outback's spellbinding skies.

AUSTRALIA
SOUTHERN LIGHTS

Chase the Southern Hemisphere's aurora australis in Tasmania.

BUDGET: $ **WHEN TO GO:** Year-round **ACTIVITY LEVEL:** Mild **GO FOR:** Aurora chasing

You've heard of the northern lights, but did you know you can chase those sky fluorescents in the Southern Hemisphere too? Spotting these elusive green and violet streaks, known as the southern lights, or aurora australis, requires a bit of luck. Like the northern lights in the Arctic, southern lights sightings are most frequent over Antarctica. But the Antarctica travel season—summer—coincides with the all-hours midnight sun. What's an aurora hunter to do?

Head to Tasmania, a landmass better positioned for aurora sightings than virtually anywhere else in the Southern Hemisphere, excluding the White Continent. Its aurora potential has to do with its geographic position and the mechanism through which auroras occur.

During solar storms, the sun flings charged particles into space. When the protons and electrons reach Earth, they congregate near the north and south geomagnetic poles, then react with the atmosphere to create ribbons of green, purple, red, or blue. Typically, the lights appear over far north or far south stretches of Earth such as Iceland or Antarctica, but when a solar storm is strong enough, you can catch them farther in toward the Equator. Tasmania, situated close to the south geomagnetic pole, is one of the hemisphere's most reliable perches.

"We have no landmass in the Southern Ocean that corresponds with Norway or Iceland," says Tasmania-based Margaret Sonnemann, author of *The Aurora Chaser's Handbook*. In the Arctic or Antarctica, where the charged particles collide with the atmosphere in the skies above, you can see the

FAST FACT

The hue of an aurora depends on where the sun's charged particles collide with Earth's atmosphere. Red auroras hit at the ionosphere, around 150 miles (240 km) high. Green streaks occur in a mildly dense stretch of the atmosphere, roughly 60 to 150 miles (100 to 240 km) from the ground. The rarer purple hues appear when the reaction strikes in our thick lower atmosphere, about 60 miles (100 km) above Earth's surface.

OPPOSITE: The aurora australis glows above Betsey Island off the southeastern coast of Tasmania.

PAGES 318-319: Take in views of Hobart from the summit of Mount Wellington.

reaction—the auroras—straight overhead. In Tasmania, you'll typically admire the show from a distance, roughly between 45 to 60 degrees on the horizon.

This vantage point offers a unique perspective. When the lights are overhead, green colors are the most noticeable, says Sonnemann. "Side on, you see the layers of color."

Given Tasmania's pristine night skies, you can spot these colorful night swirls all over the island. Look for a panorama with minimal obstructions to the southern horizon; the northern banks of a large lake looking south, or the island's southern coast looking out to sea, are ideal.

Some tried-and-true Tasmania aurora spots include Goat Bluff Lookout on the South Arm Peninsula, Carlton Beach, Tinderbox Bay, and the summit of Mount Wellington. For a southern lights–friendly hotel, try Pedder Wilderness Lodge, which has minimal light pollution and unobstructed south-facing views across Lake Pedder. Hit Taroona Beach, south of Hobart, during the warmer months to catch a thrilling after-dark duo: auroras snaking across the sky as electric blue bioluminescence pulses across the water.

One advantage of Tasmania aurora hunting: You can catch the lights year-round. Tasmania experiences nighttime darkness in every season. Though you'll have more hours of potential aurora displays in the darker winter, you could snag a stellar show on a warm summer night.

AUSTRALIA
PENGUIN PARADE

Watch hundreds of tuxedoed waddlers swim ashore.

BUDGET: $-$$ **WHEN TO GO:** November–January   **ACTIVITY LEVEL:** Mild   **GO FOR:** Wildlife

Commutes don't get much cuter than at Australia's Summerland Beach. Every evening, hundreds to thousands of skittering little penguins punch the clock on their day's work of hunting at sea—then waddle home to their protected, sandy burrows to rest up before starting the grind again.

The dusk-timed spectacle, nicknamed the "penguin parade," draws travelers from around the world to a Phillip Island beach located 88 miles (142 km) from Melbourne. It's an animal ritual that dates back thousands of years and is integral to protecting these roughly three-pound (1.4 kg) birds—the smallest known penguin species in the world.

"For safety in numbers, little penguins arrive onto land just after sunset in groups called rafts," says Paula Wasiak, a spokesperson for Phillip Island Nature Parks, noting dusk helps these penguins—which are actually white and blue, not black—avoid large predatory birds. Depending on the season, the birds might stay in the colony for just one night before hitting the sea, or for three weeks during molting, when they lose and replace their feathers.

Over the past century, local conservation organization Phillip Island Nature Parks has made this parade both accessible to onlookers and safe for penguins. The center of the action, Summerland Beach, has a tiered-seating grandstand, underground viewing area, and ranger-led hiking tours to help visitors admire and understand this pint-size species. Minimal mast lighting, erected after consultation with marine scientists, illuminates the

OPPOSITE: Little penguins have been waddling along Australia's Summerland Beach for hundreds of years.

PAGES 322-323: Watch the nightly penguin parade from the stands or ground-level observatory.

show for 50 minutes a night. That means penguins who'd rather exit the sea after dark can do so post-parade.

On a given evening, you can watch anywhere from 700 to more than 2,300 penguins shuffling at once; the record high was 5,440 penguins during the October 2022 breeding season. The island's entire colony is about 40,000 penguins strong. For the best odds of seeing the young chicks, which are no bigger than the size of a dollar bill at birth, visit from November to January, the peak season to spectate as parent penguins feed their little ones.

Tickets to this nightly event help fund conservation work to protect the penguins. Their population is stable but experiencing localized declines. The park system's work gives hope for the species' future. In the mid-1980s, the island's little penguins were predicted to go extinct by 2000. Researchers now closely monitor the species numbers. The past few decades are particularly reassuring; the number of breeding adults has jumped more than 200 percent.

FAST FACT

Can't make it to Summerland Beach in Australia? Enjoy a daily live stream of the penguin parade and a special feed of the penguins burrowing from the comfort of your couch via *penguins.org.au.*

CORAL SPAWNING DIVE

Watch the world's largest reef system reproduce.

BUDGET: $$–$$$$ **WHEN TO GO:** October–December   **ACTIVITY LEVEL:** Intermediate   **GO FOR:** Nature

Octoer kicks off one of the planet's largest reproduction events: coral spawning across the Great Barrier Reef. During the extravaganza, millions of fleck-size egg-and-sperm bundles, known as gametes, simultaneously float through the sea. Spawning is integral to the survival of these eons-old marine invertebrates—and you can see it in action on a dreamlike dusk dive.

"It's like being in a snow blizzard," says Eric Albinsson of the Professional Association of Diving Instructors (PADI), although instead of powdery snowflakes, you're swarmed by "millions of tiny pinkish dots." Coral polyps across the reef system pump out these tiny blush-hued packages at the same time. As the bundles float around, they bump into gametes of the same species and fertilize. Once the deed is done, the bundles sink back down to plant themselves in the seafloor, where they can grow roughly four inches (10 cm) a year.

Mass spawning is essential for species survival; gametes only have a few viable hours for reproduction. The sheer volume also minimizes the number of eggs predators can consume.

Scientists only discovered the existence of coral spawning in the 1980s. The process requires Goldilocks-like conditions. The water currents and temperature need to be just right—roughly 72°F (22°C) or higher for the

FAST FACT

Given the Great Barrier Reef's enormity, only 10 percent of it can be regularly monitored for climate change effects. That's why researchers launched the Great Reef Census, a citizen science effort to collect data from the ocean. To partake, submit your Great Barrier Reef photos online at *greatreefcensus.org*.

OPPOSITE: Coral spawning is necessary for the future of the Great Barrier Reef.

PAGES 326-327: There are more than 600 species of corals and 1,500 species of fish in the protected areas of the Great Barrier Reef.

month leading up to spawning—with a full moon overhead. Even with perfect conditions, it can be tough to predict when the reproduction will happen.

You can dive the mass spawning phenomenon in waterways around the globe, but nothing compares to the Great Barrier Reef. In Queensland, Australia, the close-to-shore reefs typically welcome the spectacle in the days following the October full moon. Farther offshore, the mass spawning begins after the November or December full moons. Spawning often takes place two to three hours after sunset, but sightings are never guaranteed.

Most dive trips depart from Cairns, a gateway to the Great Barrier Reef. Give yourself the flexibility of multiple days to improve your odds of catching this nighttime marvel. A PADI open water certification is required, and a night dive certification is recommended. If you aren't certified, some dive shops welcome snorkelers too. Gearwise, cover up in a wet suit with a hood to protect your ears.

WHERE TO STAY

Lady Elliot Island Eco Resort, located at the Great Barrier Reef's southern tip, is a case study in sustainable hospitality. The 44-room lodge runs entirely on renewable energy and operates regular reef health surveys. The property's owners have joined the local community to help revegetate much of the island. On-site research projects also help protect the area's many species, including manta rays and nesting sea turtles.

Coral spawning astounds recreational divers. For conservationists, the process also presents an opportunity: Throughout the Great Barrier Reef, which spans approximately 134,360 square miles (348,000 km²), corals face increasing threats from climate change. The reef has lost more than half of its coral over the past three decades, and warming ocean temperatures have sparked multiple mass bleaching events.

Scientists with the Great Barrier Reef Foundation now run coral IVF conservation procedures timed to the spawning events. They collect coral eggs and sperm during reproduction events, place the gametes in a floating pool to fertilize, then replant the babies onto damaged stretches of the reef floor. Early signs show this strategy is working. In fact, the first Great Barrier Reef coral IVF plantings survived a major bleaching event and grew to maturity, eventually spawning to produce their own coral babies.

AUSTRALIA

GLOWING FUNGI

Take a walk on the wild side down Ghost Mushroom Lane.

BUDGET: $ **WHEN TO GO:** May–June **ACTIVITY LEVEL:** Intermediate **GO FOR:** Nature

I f the idea of a forest carpeted with glowing mushrooms sounds far-fetched, you've never been to Ghost Mushroom Lane. This pine forest attraction on South Australia's Limestone Coast supports an abundance of *Omphalotus nidiformis*, better known as ghost fungus. Beneath the sun, the species looks like your average fungi. Come twilight, the colorful mushrooms emit an ethereal lime green glow.

The ground dwellers are common in Australia, with the largest numbers in Tasmania and South Australia. Ghost Mushroom Lane, located near the town of Glencoe in South Australia, is known for its proliferation of the fungi. The destination hosts a web of short trails that weave by marked points with clusters of the glowing mushrooms. You can tackle these mild jaunts on your own, or learn the ins and outs of the forest's mycology via a tour with a local guide.

Like fireflies and jellyfish, ghost mushrooms produce their own light through a chemical reaction of luciferin and oxygen. At its brightest, you could read a book by the light this species can produce. The clustered fungi, roughly eight inches (20 cm) each, congregate on rotting logs and stumps. They resemble oyster mushrooms, but take caution: Ghost fungi are toxic. These are not mushrooms you want to taste.

May and June (late fall into winter in the Southern Hemisphere) are the best months to catch the incandescence on Ghost Mushroom Lane, located

OPPOSITE: Ghost mushrooms are most typically found on tree trunks and rotting wood.

PAGES 332-333: Known as ghost fungi, these poisonous mushrooms are most commonly found in southern Australia and Tasmania.

near the town of Glencoe. Plan your trip around a new moon when the skies are darker; a bright, fuller moon will obscure the green tinge.

Don't get discouraged if you can't see the color right away; your eyes need roughly 20 minutes to get used to the darkness (a red flashlight will expedite vision adjustments). Try long-exposure photography to see the glow at its most vivid.

The *Omphalotus nidiformis* is one of the best known glowing mushroom species, but around 80 species of fungi use bioluminescence. Scientists still don't know why they shine—some mycologists believe it's an unintentional by-product of the chemical reaction rather than an evolutionary necessity—yet we do know they've been wowing scientists and onlookers for centuries. Aristotle was among the first to share a terrestrial bioluminescence sighting, which he called "glowing wood." Of course, Indigenous Australians knew about the phenomenon well before that. Some associated the spectacle with evil spirits, whereas others saw it as an occurrence from the supernatural world.

WHILE YOU'RE THERE

South Australia's Mount Gambier brims with mystery, from glowing fungi to striking sinkholes. After you get your shroom fix, head 20 minutes south to snorkel or scuba dive the 200-foot-deep (60 m) crystal clear waters of Kilsby, named one of the world's best sinkhole dive sites for its sharp visibility and ethereal beams of light.

AUSTRALIA

CLIMB A BRIDGE AT NIGHT

Tackle Sydney's famous ascent after dark.

BUDGET: $$$ **WHEN TO GO:** Year-round   **ACTIVITY LEVEL:** Intermediate   **GO FOR:** Adventure

Clamber up Australia's steel giant, the Sydney Harbour Bridge, to see its namesake city shimmer like a jewelry box. Outfitter Bridge-Climb takes travelers up and over the architectural marvel—the tallest steel arch bridge in the world. Many traipse the steps, catwalks, and stairs to the bridge's 440-foot (134 m) summit for 360-degree Sydney views throughout the day. A moonlit climb ups the ante—and awe.

Thrill seekers don their climbing garb (a gray bodysuit), fasten their safety harness belts and headlamps, then clip in at the bridge base as early evening's peachy glow descends. It's a steady, but leisurely, ascent above the whizzing roadway below. Within two hours, you'll reach the summit and watch as sunset's golden hour turns to night. Illuminated icons across Sydney Harbour, such as the famed sail-topped opera house, shimmer beneath the midnight blue sky.

To see the Sydney Harbour in kaleidoscopic splendor, time your trip to Vivid Sydney, a three-week festival of light, music, and innovation that runs from May to June. BridgeClimb hosts a Vivid Sydney Climb, a nightly jaunt that gives travelers a bird's-eye view of the festival's magic. Fantastical light projections bathe the skyline, Rocks and Darling harbors, and the opera house, in neon hues.

The BridgeClimb experience spans roughly three and a half hours and is doable for anyone with moderate fitness. Book tickets in advance, particularly for the Vivid Sydney Climb, as slots sell out quickly.

OPPOSITE: For the most breathtaking views of Sydney Harbour, climb its bridge at night.

NEW ZEALAND
NIGHT CANYONING

Go spelunking beneath the North Island stars.

BUDGET: $$$ WHEN TO GO: Year-round   ACTIVITY LEVEL: Strenuous   GO FOR: Adventure

As wet suit–clad day hikers exit New Zealand's Piha Canyon before sunset, night canyoneers know their adventure has only just begun. This lush rainforest, a North Island medley of black sand shores, towering cliffs, and deep caves, is one of few places in the world to try spelunking after dark. It's a night of waterfall abseiling, caving, wild swimming, and adrenaline-pumping jumps—with nothing but a headlamp and the cosmos to light your way. "It's different at night; the headlamps illuminate rock features like a moonscape," says Cam Bowen of AWOL Canyoning Adventures, the outfitter that runs this hair-raising excursion.

Eye-popping rocks aren't the only otherworldly sight on this two-hour canyoning jaunt. After completing step one—rappelling under a waterfall—you'll squeeze into, then swim through, a water-seeped cave that has dozens of glitzy teal glowworms bejeweling the rocky ceiling like constellations. It's a taste of the splendor at another North Island stunner: Waitomo Caves, where travelers flock to see thousands of the sparkly larvae by day.

The Piha Canyon excursion, located 25 miles (40 km) from Auckland in the Waitakere Ranges rainforest, runs year-round. It begins with a 30-minute forest walk at sunset. You'll reach the canyon entrance by dusk, tighten your provided gear—a harness, wet suit, helmet, and headlamp—then leap into the dusky abyss. This is a guided excursion only and requires good physical fitness, and being comfortable in tight, dark places is recommended.

OPPOSITE: Glowworm-dotted caves are a staple New Zealand experience, and you can enjoy them by boat in Waitomo Caves (pictured) or by spelunking in Piha Canyon.

WAIRARAPA DARK SKY RESERVE

Discover the world's growing dark sky movement at this stargazing hub.

BUDGET: $–$$$ **WHEN TO GO:** Year-round   **ACTIVITY LEVEL:** Mild   **GO FOR:** Stargazing

Stargazing is a staple of any New Zealand adventure, but few destinations illustrate the country's Indigenous Maori-led dark sky movement like Wairarapa Dark Sky Reserve on the North Island. This 1,415-square-mile (3,665 km²) reserve, roughly the size of Rhode Island, lies around 90 minutes from capital city Wellington. Its jet-black skies are dark enough to observe deep space objects, including the Tarantula Nebula, a spot in a distant galaxy where stars are formed, as well as near-nightly glimpses of the Milky Way and its dynamic core.

Nightscape protections like Wairarapa's are integral to the country's goal to gain DarkSky International's certification as a Dark Sky Nation. And New Zealand is already well on its way: There are two DarkSky International Dark Sky Reserves within the country, and the vast majority of night skies across the North and South Islands are considered pristine or with minimal degradation at the horizon.

The final hurdle to Dark Sky Nation status requires virtually everyone in New Zealand to get on board with nightscape-protective changes, such as lighting adjustments. That's where easily reachable sites like Wairarapa, close to Wellington's population of 540,000 (roughly 11 percent of New Zealand's population) come into play. "To institutionalize dark skies, we need to change the hearts and minds of people," says Haritina Mogoşanu, a Wairarapa-based

ASTRONOMICAL WONDERS

In 2020, the Pacific island of Niue made history as the world's first Dark Sky Nation, as certified by Dark-Sky International. This stargazing oasis is accessible via flights from Auckland, with Niuean guides who intimately know the Pacific's night skies available to lead astronomy tours.

OPPOSITE: The Milky Way rises above Kaikōura Beach on New Zealand's South Island.

PAGES 340-341: Wairarapa's unpolluted skies mean crystal clear galaxy views from nearly every vantage point in the reserve.

astrobiologist who helped the reserve gain Dark-Sky certification in 2023.

A main impetus for the country's light-pollution reduction is to preserve Maori culture, which for centuries has been interlinked with the islands' nightscapes. Maori ancestors arrived in Aotearoa (modern-day New Zealand) millennia ago via celestial navigation, says Rangi Mātāmua, a Maori astronomer of Ngāi Tūhoe descent. Constellations and the moon dictated when to hunt or fish and when trees would flower. Maori people and places were named after interstellar objects, and cultural star stories were passed down through generations.

Preserving these splendid skies isn't just an opportunity for nightly stargazing, but also insurance that future generations understand and carry on their ancestors' stories. Losing the ability to see interstellar objects would "diminish the culture," says Mātāmua.

While many of the world's best loved stargazing spots are found in remote escapes, Wairarapa proves communities and cities can preserve their

WHILE YOU'RE THERE

Aoraki Mackenzie International Dark Sky Reserve pairs stargazing and wellness with astonishing hot springs soaks. On this guided 90-minute experience, available at Tekapo Springs, you'll tour the nightscape via telescope. Then look at the stars from a floating hammock or raft in a 100°F (38°C) natural hot pool.

ABOVE: Find unbelievable stargazing from the beaches on Castlepoint, a settlement on the Wairarapa coast on New Zealand's North Island.

OPPOSITE: Castlepoint Lighthouse stands 171 feet (52 m) above the coastline.

night skies too. The reserve is a blend of bucolic countryside, vineyards, residential towns, and the Aorangi Forest Park, which covers the island's southern stretch. To earn DarkSky status, Wairarapa-area residents joined forces with local councils, organizations, and businesses to turn the region into a stargazing success story—one where astrotourism options now abound.

Though Aorangi Forest Park boasts the area's darkest skies, you'll have dazzling twilight views just about anywhere in the reserve. Local outfitter Under the Stars brings astronomy right to your doorstep, offering a private, guided stargazing session via telescope in your hotel or vacation rental's backyard.

Mogosanu and her partner run astronomy experiences via Star Safari, an observation center with some of Wairarapa's most powerful telescopes. During these 90-minute sessions, you'll spot star clusters, galaxies, and even a quasar (an enormous black hole that sucks in gas).

ANTARCTICA

WHITE CONTINENT CAMPING

Sleep within reach of the South Pole—and penguins.

BUDGET: $$$$$ **WHEN TO GO:** November–January   **ACTIVITY LEVEL:** Intermediate   **GO FOR:** Adventure

A visit to Antarctica tops many travel wish lists, but there's a way to take the once-in-a-lifetime experience up a notch. Instead of sleeping on a cruise ship—the accommodation for most Antarctica travelers—try a night of camping on the continent's sparkly white shores. If you plan your trip right, you can even stay up late to admire the midnight sun's glow with the sound of cracking ice in the background.

The first option: Book an expedition cruise. Cruising is the main mode of travel for Antarctica tourism, and many outfitters, particularly ones with smaller ships, offer guests a one-night sleep on the ice, which is often available via lottery. It's a welcome respite after the harrowing journey through Drake Passage, a washing machine stretch of ocean that connects the southernmost tip of South America, Cape Horn, with Antarctica's South Shetland Islands (and the part of the journey most likely to leave visitors seasick). Although sleeping on the edge of the planet is hardly a five-star experience, the jaw-dropping night is worth the frigid temperatures and wind.

"It was unlike any other camping experience," says travel writer and photographer Lauren Breedlove, who slept on the White Continent with outfitter Hurtigruten. "When the glacier wasn't calving, the wind wasn't blowing, and everyone was sleeping, it was the most deafening silence I've ever heard." The overnight site changes throughout the season; sometimes

OPPOSITE: Only the most intrepid travelers have the chance to make camp on Antarctica's shores.

PAGES 346-347: Directional signposts point the way to destinations beyond the White Continent from the Dome C outpost.

campers find themselves lying within earshot of a chatting penguin colony—the surefire recipe for an adorable, and sleepless, night.

Your evening of Antarctic overnighting begins after dinner on the ship. You'll hit the bathroom one last time, then depart to your snow patch via skiff or Zodiac boat. An expedition guide helps you set up in either a tent or a weatherproof bivouac bag, the cocoon-like choice of many soldiers and mountaineers. It's a roughly 10-hour outing, and one where the sun never sets. White Continent camping happens in time with the Southern Hemisphere's midnight sun.

Come morning, it's time to head back to the boat for a warm-up with piping hot coffee. "The Zodiac ride back to the ship in the morning was a highlight," says Breedlove. "The water was calm with reflections of the mountains and icebergs."

Cruising isn't the only way to enjoy a night on ice. Union Glacier Camp, a full-service private camp that runs during the Antarctic summer, can house up to 70 visitors in double-walled clam tents. The camp sits in an enviable location:

WHILE YOU'RE THERE

Brag to your future self about your wild night on ice with a postcard sent from Port Lockroy research station, one of Antarctica's most visited sites. The station gathers and sends travelers' postmarked mail but be ready for a wait: It can take more than a month for your letter to reach the mainland. Most cruise vessels make a stop at the station.

ABOVE: During the day, take a Zodiac boat to explore the ice formations, glaciers, and icebergs surrounding the White Continent.

OPPOSITE: You may wake up to the sounds of a penguin colony happily huddled just outside your tent.

roughly 600 nautical miles (965 km) from the true South Pole. Given its extreme remoteness, the journey to reach Union Glacier Camp is a sightseeing adventure in and of itself. You'll fly from Punta Arenas, Chile, to a naturally occurring blue ice runway—a sturdy but slick stretch of ice, where it feels like your plane could spin out at any moment.

Once you've arrived on this ivory expanse, all sorts of adventures await: hiking, cross-country skiing, fat-tire biking, or a chartered flightseeing trip around the neighboring Ellsworth Mountains or the base camp of Mount Vinson, Antarctica's highest peak. You'll enjoy freshly cooked meals in the community mess tent, with evening talks on polar history and geology. Despite the cold, windy weather, typically between minus 12° and 30°F (−24° and −1°C), you can rest assured your nylon-covered tent will remain naturally heated to a warm 60°F (16°C), thanks to the around-the-clock sun.

CELESTIAL NAVIGATION

Follow the sky like a Polynesian wayfinder.

BUDGET: $$ **WHEN TO GO:** Year-round   **ACTIVITY LEVEL:** Intermediate   **GO FOR:** Culture

S tars were a compass for one of mankind's most awe-inspiring migrations. More than 3,000 years ago, well before the arrival of navigational aids like sextants, Polynesian seafarers used the moon, sun, constellations, and wind to journey across the Pacific. That tradition of wayfinding has been passed down through generations and continues today. Learn about the craft and try it for yourself, with an introduction to celestial navigation led by Polynesian voyager and native Tahitian Tahiarii Pariente, who uses these tours to show an important side of Polynesian culture—one that helped him rediscover and embrace his own roots.

Millennia ago, Polynesian navigators traveled hundreds of miles across the Pacific, aboard double-hulled canoes known as *va'a*. By around A.D. 1000, these wayfinders had settled more than 1,000 islands in the Polynesian Triangle, which links New Zealand, Hawaii, and Easter Island across 10 million square miles (25,900,000 km2) of ocean.

It's a courageous history with astonishing navigational feats, but for decades European and U.S. colonizers scrubbed Polynesian voyaging records from history books. The result was that young Tahitians and Hawaiians were taught that their ancestors aimlessly drifted, then settled the islands. To colonizers, noninstrumental navigation sounded impossible.

Things changed in the 1970s when the Polynesian Voyaging Society (PVS),

OPPOSITE: On the island of Taha'a, palm trees stand tall beneath a clear view of the Milky Way.

PAGES 352-353: The landscape seems magical as the sun sets over a lagoon in front of a resort in Moorea.

based in Hawaii, set out to disprove the naysayers. These Hawaii Natives, who were trained in voyaging, sailed from Hawaii to Tahiti without navigational tools to prove the history books wrong and to preserve their cherished tradition.

The arrival of that first Hawaiian va'a on the shores of Tahiti in the 1970s sparked a newfound sense of pride across the Pacific. Native Tahitians like Pariente, founder of tour outfitter Polynesian Escape, felt called to learn the craft.

Pariente trained with the PVS in Hawaii for nearly a decade before bringing his knowledge back home to Tahiti. He now runs cultural tours year-round from Tahiti, Bora-Bora, and his home island, Raiatea. One of his most important excursions takes place beneath the cosmos: celestial navigation. "I explain the story and foundation of how we became what we are," Pariente says of the experience.

These introductory tours about wayfinding, which run on land and water, teach travelers about

OTHER MARVELS

The island of Raiatea, a 20-minute flight from Bora-Bora, is home to UNESCO World Heritage site Taputapuātea marae, one of Polynesia's most sacred places. This meeting ground, constructed between the 14th to 18th centuries, was a political, ceremonial, and spiritual center of eastern Polynesia. Everyone from elders to dignitaries met here to honor their ancestors. Navigators also launched and concluded their voyages in the marae, which is now open to tourists.

ABOVE: The crew of the *Hōkūle'a* trains in the ancient art of Polynesian wayfinding—navigating without modern tools. In 2023, they embarked on a circumnavigation of the Pacific.

OPPOSITE: Polynesian sailors once used reeds to create nautical navigational maps.

the islands' rich sailing tradition, as well as how to see the sky like a navigator. Ancient Polynesian wayfinders looked to the constellations as guardrails; they broke the sky into quadrants to determine directions based on where constellations rose and set. For example, one key signpost, the Southern Cross, has a line of two stars that point in the direction of the South Pole, similar to the Northern Hemisphere's North Star. Wayfinders also created stick charts, constructed from materials like palm ribs, shells, and coral pebbles to identify patterns of ocean conditions and the direction of swells.

Though Pariente's tours last several hours, he can only scratch the surface of the lifelong wayfinding craft, but the celestial navigation trips help visitors understand Polynesian culture on a deeper level. "Culture is defined by the relationship between individuals and the environment," he says. "Here, there's ocean, water, marine species, birds, and the sky."

SAMOA

PALOLO HUNTING

Fish at twilight to bring in Samoa's squiggly blue sea worms.

BUDGET: $$ **WHEN TO GO:** October   **ACTIVITY LEVEL:** Intermediate   **GO FOR:** Nature

Stars swim through the sky as swarms of net-toting Samoans wade into the inky sea. Overhead, a nearly full waning gibbous moon radiates with a reminder: The wriggly palolo worms may soon be within reach. This scene is the start of a late-night Samoan tradition known as the palolo hunt, a time to catch the delectable South Pacific sea worm that only appears once or twice a year.

The typically bright blue palolo, a 16-inch (40 cm) polychaete worm, spends most of its life burrowed into the corals of shallow reefs. Roughly seven nights after the October full moon and potentially again after the November full moon, the palolos spawn and create quite the spectacle.

With their heads nestled in the corals, the worms launch their spaghetti-shaped rear ends, called epitokes, toward the sky. These strands carry egg- and sperm-filled sacs that burst at the water's surface. Like corals, the epitokes' release sparks a mass spawning event—and the start of Samoa's palolo harvest, an annual long-standing and sacred cultural tradition dedicated to these savory worms.

"Our people believed this was a special god that came from the ocean," says Taioaliiseu Taimalelagi Saunia Afoa Fiti Aimaasu, a Samoan high chief and owner of tour outfitter Tai's Native Experience. The Samoans built their prehistoric calendar around the worms. "There was the pre-palolo season, and post-palolo season." It's likewise a significant moment for other South Pacific islands known to have palolo occurrences, such as Vanuatu.

Tours to join this twilight angling trip and to taste the fishy worm, described

OTHER MARVELS

See another side of the Samoan sea at the protected Palolo Deep Marine Reserve just beyond the capital city of Apia. The blue hole astounds snorkelers and divers with sheer walls of rainbow-hued corals, as well as the clown triggerfish, reef sharks, and sea turtles that frequent them.

OPPOSITE: Polynesian fire dancing, also known as fire knife dancing, is rooted in ancient Samoan practices.

PAGES 358-359: Come daylight, explore Samoa's beautiful white sand beaches backed by verdant mountain peaks.

as the "caviar of the Pacific," begin in the capital city of Apia, located on Upolu island. It's an early wake-up call, with a 3 a.m. pickup. You'll drive an hour outside Apia to the rural coastlines, then join a packed crowd of shore-perched Samoans waiting for the hunt to begin. "It's a whole rugby field of people on the beach just waiting for the worm to rise," says Aimaasu, noting the atmosphere is welcoming and lively. "Even if the palolo doesn't appear, just being out there with local people is different."

The act of catching the palolo, known as *ka palolo,* requires a net and a bright flashlight or lantern. Each epitoke section has a small eyespot that's drawn to light; palolo hunters use lanterns to strategically attract them. Another trick of the ka palolo trade: Wear a sweet-scented moso'oi flower lei—Samoans say the fragrance attracts the worms.

A twilight pickup, a handmade lei, traipsing into the sea by moonlight—that's a lot of work for a little worm. According to Aimaasu, it's well worth it. The rich-tasting worm is a delicacy among Samoans. When traditionally prepared, palolo is fried in butter, cooked with onions, and served on toasted sandwiches. Alternatively, you can try the worm raw.

The palolo hunt is becoming less predictable though. The worm is listed on the IUCN Red List of threatened species, with concerns it could go extinct due to stressors affecting coral reefs and marine species. "I remember as a kid, it usually came in abundance," says Aimaasu. "Now, it doesn't come some years."

PART SIX

SOUTH AMERICA

The Milky Way rises above the Pomerape (left) and Parinacota (right) volcanoes and the Cotacotani Lagoons in Arica, Chile.

VENDIMIA FESTIVAL

Sip some of the world's best vino during Mendoza's autumn harvest celebration.

BUDGET: $-$$ **WHEN TO GO:** Early March **ACTIVITY LEVEL:** Mild **GO FOR:** Culture

A s the world's fifth largest wine-producing country, Argentina takes its grapes seriously—but not too seriously. In early March, the country applauds its yields, and the farmers and vintners behind its beloved vines, with the action-packed Vendimia harvest festival in Mendoza.

The world-renowned autumn event delights Argentines with a string of nighttime fanfare. The festivities begin the first Friday of March with an evening beauty pageant parade to select the Reina Nacional de la Vendimia (harvest queen). Dozens of contestants from Mendoza Province dress up to represent their districts, with floats and attire paying homage to their home's renowned fruits.

Saturday night brings the ultimate extravaganza. Some 25,000 revelers gather in the Frank Romero Day Greek Amphitheater for the harvest festival's main act: the crowning of the harvest queen. Live music, local wines, and multicolored light shows set the stage for the naming. Fireworks, costumes, dancing, and free-flowing wine follow the announcement and then last well into the night. The celebrations repeat over the subsequent two nights.

In 2003, the government of Mendoza formalized a new addition to its festival: Vendimia Para Todos (Vendimia for Everyone), an LGBTQIA+ harvest festival, with its own grape harvest queen.

OPPOSITE: The harvest queen is crowned to great fanfare, with light shows and pyrotechnics.

SALAR DE UYUNI

See the stars reflected in every direction.

BUDGET: $$-$$$$ **WHEN TO GO:** January–March   **ACTIVITY LEVEL:** Mild   **GO FOR:** Stargazing

When rainy season hits Bolivia's Salar de Uyuni, the 4,050-square-mile (10,500 km²) salt flat transforms into a space portal—at least, it looks that way by night.

A thin layer of precipitation turns the crusty desert floor into a real-life planetarium. "It's like a giant cosmic mirror that reflects the night sky above," says Gijs Dijkshoorn, co-founder of Bolivia-based Ruta Verde Tours. "You see the whole sky at your feet."

A Salar de Uyuni stargazing tour is your ticket to an out-of-this-world experience. The expanse, which contains 10 billion tons (9 billion t) of salt and about 70 percent of the world's lithium, was once covered by a prehistoric lake. Now, this amalgam of paper white polygons dazzles astrotourists with pristine peeks into outer space.

At an elevation of around 12,000 feet (3,650 m) above sea level in Bolivia's Altiplano region, you're a touch closer to space too. And to top it off, the area has virtually no light pollution. You can see Magellanic Clouds, star clusters, and distant galaxies in the pristine dark skies. The Milky Way glimmers above the salt flat year-round, with February through late October providing the best views of the eye-popping core of our galaxy.

To see the salt floor reflect the cosmos, visit during the rainy season from December to April; January through March specifically offer the best

OPPOSITE: **The night sky reflects on the salt flats, a charming illusion that makes it seem like the stars are at your feet.**

PAGES 366-367: **Uyuni is the world's largest salt flat, with more than 10 billion tons (9 billion t) of salt across its expanse.**

precipitation odds. Just a light precipitation layer is required to create the astronomical reflections—a sensation that feels like you're "floating in outer space," says Dijkshoorn, who runs salt-flat stargazing trips year-round.

Tours typically pair golden hour with cosmic exploration, whether a predawn-to-sunrise outing or a sunset-to-nightfall excursion. For the ultimate treat, book a camper van trip to sleep under the stars right on the salt flat.

Though the night sky is the star of the Salar de Uyuni show, you'll find plenty to do come daylight. Visit Isla Incahuasi, a cactus-studded expanse atop an ancient volcano, for a geological history lesson. When the salt flat was a lake, this volcano was actually an island. Now, it's a perch overlooking the vast white terrain. Other nearby stops include Laguna Colorada, a striking red lake, and Laguna Verde, a teal green lake at the base of the Licancabur volcano.

WHERE TO STAY

See the salt, then sleep in it, at Hotel Palacio de Sal, the world's first luxury salt hotel—as in, a hotel made entirely from salt. (Think ice hotel, but salt!) It took more than a million salt bricks to construct this sleek 30-room property, which welcomes guests on the edge of Salar de Uyuni.

DÍA DE LAS VELITAS

Partake in Colombia's annual night of candlelight.

BUDGET: $ **WHEN TO GO:** December 7   **ACTIVITY LEVEL:** Mild   **GO FOR:** Culture

Colombia is even more enchanting during the countrywide Día de las Velitas celebration. As the Day of the Little Candles gets under way, main squares, tucked-away alleys, and homes flicker with the flames of countless candles set ablaze. The cheer and frivolity happen annually on the night of December 7 and, in many destinations, last well into morning. It's part of the country's Immaculate Conception merriment that dates back more than a century.

In 1854, Pope Pius IX declared the Immaculate Conception—the belief that the Virgin Mary was free from original sin—as dogma in the Catholic faith. Catholics in Rome and around the world lit candles in a vigil the evening before the December 8, 1854, decision. Colombia has continued the tradition for more than 100 years, and people of all faiths are invited to join in.

Outfitters like Colombian Buddy offer Día de las Velitas tours to help travelers join the fun, including a night of traditional celebrations with local families. The holiday experience varies by location, with nearly every city in the country participating. Several destinations go particularly above and beyond.

One of the best known Día de las Velitas gatherings is in Quimbaya, a municipality in western Colombia. Quimbaya neighbors vie for the most spectacular light display as part of their annual Candles and Lanterns Festival,

OPPOSITE: Día de las Velitas celebrates the beginning of the Christmas season.

PAGES 370-371: Along with candles in homes and stores, many streets are filled with intricate, illuminated paper lanterns.

timed to Día de las Velitas. Communities from across more than 100 blocks rally together for two nights of friendly competition. The festival runs December 7 to 8, with some 20,000 glimmering lanterns, plus food stalls and cultural experiences throughout town.

Barranquilla, located near the country's northwest coast, is another Día de las Velitas fan favorite—and the gaiety is known to get rowdy. Street parties run from evening until around 3 a.m. Revelers light their home and street candles, then stay up until sunrise to welcome the Christmas season.

Milder, more family-focused experiences take place in cities like Bogotá. Here, Colombians light candles in their homes, then join together with loved ones for a feast of *natilla* (a sweet custard treat), *buñuelos* (crispy fritters), and the traditional main course: *lechona* (suckling pig). Though the Bogotá events center on family, celebrators still fill the city spaces with candles and *farolitos* (paper lanterns), plus take part in traditional music and dancing that lasts past dark.

FAST FACT

For six weeks, Medellín is adorned with millions of holiday lights during El Alumbrado Navideño. More than 100 locations, including the particularly festive Medellín River area, celebrate the Christmas lighting festival, which commences after Día de las Velitas.

ATACAMA DESERT STARGAZING

Admire the cosmos from one of Earth's darkest and driest deserts.

BUDGET: $$-$$$ **WHEN TO GO:** Year-round   **ACTIVITY LEVEL:** Mild   **GO FOR:** Stargazing

Astrotourists aren't the only ones gawking at the polka-dotted nightscapes in Chile's arid Atacama Desert. This stargazing haven, the driest nonpolar desert on Earth, is home to some of the astronomy world's most powerful and important telescopes—not to mention a host of space-seeking options for travelers.

With high elevation and minimal precipitation or cloud cover, the Atacama Desert boasts the perfect conditions for surveilling outer space. That's why many astronomical authorities set up shop here. The Atacama Large Millimeter/submillimeter Array, known as ALMA, uses some of Earth's most advanced telescopes to study how the universe and planets first formed. Another Atacama astronomy hub, the Paranal Observatory, monitors black holes and dark matter. Its findings have helped astronomers study the potential black hole at the center of our own galaxy.

Though the scientific discoveries are astounding, you don't need high-end credentials to enjoy Atacama's inky skies. Many observatories, including ALMA and Paranal, welcome travelers by day, while trained local guides host all sorts of niche stargazing tours come nightfall, from astrophotography to Indigenous sky-watching.

After dark, learn about Southern Hemisphere constellations and admire galaxies and deep space objects with Jorge Corante, founder of Atacama

OPPOSITE: **Jupiter can be seen along with the Large Magellanic Cloud above the Miscanti volcano in the Atacama Desert.**

PAGES 374-375: **The Atacama Large Millimeter/submillimeter Array is one of the most complex observatories in the world.**

Desert Stargazing. Corante was part of the team that built ALMA in the early 2000s. Now, the Chilean guide and night sky buff runs tours on his own private observatory near San Pedro de Atacama. Evenings with Corante's high-powered telescopes can last anywhere from three hours to all night long. Most hotels in the San Pedro de Atacama area, such as Awasi Atacama, run stargazing trips via private observatories too.

To experiment with astrophotography, book an outing with local photographer Mauro Cuevas, founder of 3K Private Tours. Cuevas leads private night sky photography excursions in Vallecito, an otherworldly erosion-carved landscape that overlooks the distant snowcapped Andes. It's a destination that feels more like Mars than Earth—which isn't all that surprising, given NASA uses the desert as a training ground in its search for life on the red planet.

If cultural stargazing sounds intriguing, head just south of the desert to Elqui Valley for an evening of archaeoastronomy with Astro Elqui. This locally run observatory pairs skygazing with the

OTHER MARVELS

When rains are heavy enough, an explosion of magenta flowers carpet a southern swath of Chile's Atacama Desert. The region's new Desierto Florido National Park, created in 2023, provides a front-row seat to the blossoms, not to mention the impressive nightscapes this rugged desert is known for.

Indigenous Diaguita culture's stories of the cosmos. You'll learn these night sky tales while enjoying music and snacks by the campfire. Elqui Valley is also home to the 88,900-acre (36,000 ha) Gabriela Mistral Dark Sky Sanctuary, a stargazing hub certified by DarkSky International in northern Chile's wine region. This was the world's first official Dark Sky Sanctuary. To see it at its most dazzling, book a night at Elqui Domos, a wilderness accommodation with an astronomical observatory and after-dark tours like trekking or horse-back rides.

The Atacama has an average of 300 clear, cloud-free nights a year. Visiting just before, during, or after a new moon is best for the darkest skies and most dramatic starscapes. It may be a desert, but don't forget to pack layers—nights in the Atacama can get chilly, particularly in the shoulder seasons and winter.

AMAZON NIGHT CANOEING

Listen as this world-renowned rainforest gets raucous after dark.

BUDGET: $$$$–$$$$$ **WHEN TO GO:** Year-round   **ACTIVITY LEVEL:** Intermediate   **GO FOR:** Wildlife

S unset triggers a distinct changing of the animal kingdom guards in the Amazon rainforest. Diurnal creatures hoot and howl their final messages of the day, while nocturnal rainforest dwellers, such as frogs and owls, stir from their daily slumber. "The moment they wake up, it's this boom, like an explosion of sound that fills the entire forest," says Ecuadorian scientist Jarol Fernando Vaca.

To hear the forest change for yourself, board a canoe for a riotous night paddle. Properties throughout the Amazon run nightly guided canoe trips to help guests experience one of the jungle's busiest transitional moments: dusk. These eerie outings will awaken your senses—from echoing frog croaks to shimmering yellow caiman eyes that have been trained on you since that first oar stroke, whether or not you knew it.

Any Amazon night outing will delight, but there's nothing like canoeing through the kapok-dotted Yasuní Biosphere Reserve, a UNESCO World Heritage site. With steady rainfall and its location at the junction of the Andes Mountains, the Amazon River, and the Equator, Yasuní is one of the most biodiverse places on the planet. In fact, more species of frogs and toads are native to this region than in the United States and Canada combined. The reserve boasts nearly 600 bird species, more than 150 types of amphibians, around 200 species of mammals, and an astonishing 100,000 unique insect species.

WHILE YOU'RE THERE

For an extra special safari, try the canopy crane at Sacha Lodge. This project, launched in 2023, is the Amazon's first canopy crane (it looks like a construction crane), and one of just a dozen in the world.

OPPOSITE: Parrots gather around a clay lick at the Napo Wildlife Center in Yasuní National Park.

PAGES 380-381: From the bromeliads, ferns, and orchids that cover a kapok tree to the jaguars that prowl below, Yasuní National Park is home to countless plants and animal species.

Evening paddle trips across black-water lakes and creeks lend an auditory perspective. "It's important to listen," says Vaca, who also works as a guide for Sacha Lodge, a property located in the Yasuní Biosphere Reserve that runs these after-dark outings. "Most of the time you don't see a lot of the action, but you can listen to it."

The canoe trips, which typically depart after dinner, run for two to three hours, accompanied by scientific information about the chirps and calls that surround you. Though hearing may be the dominant sense, rest assured you'll see plenty of critters too, be they caimans, frogs, bats, or the shimmery glowworms that dot the waterway's lily pads.

In addition to the twilight paddle trips, many Amazon lodges host nighttime jungle treks to shed more light on this biodiverse ecosystem. Night hikes run for several hours, with a chance to spot even more forest dwellers, such as snakes, tarantulas, sleeping birds, and—if you're particularly lucky—more elusive inhabitants like giant anteaters.

Most trips to the Yasuní Biosphere Reserve require at least four days. The journey begins with a flight to Coca, the Ecuadorian Amazon gateway, followed by a multi-hour boat ride, then a canoe jaunt, to reach your accommodation. Quito, Ecuador's capital, is the easiest jumping-off point to reach Coca.

AN INCA PLANETARIUM

Stargaze like the ancient astronomers at Planetarium Cusco.

BUDGET: $ **WHEN TO GO:** Year-round   **ACTIVITY LEVEL:** Mild   **GO FOR:** Stargazing

T he Inca civilization accomplished many world-renowned feats, from erecting 25,000 miles (40,230 km) of rugged-terrain roads to constructing engineering marvels like Machu Picchu. In Peru, Planetarium Cusco celebrates another well-harnessed skill of the Inca civilization: astronomy.

Visits to the planetarium, located just outside Cusco, are broken into three stages: Your trip begins in the interpretation center, where artwork and narration illustrate how the Inca people relied on the sky from around A.D. 1200 to 1500. The Inca people used constellations and solar observatories to monitor the changing seasons and agricultural milestones. Their economy hinged on farming; studying the movement of the stars and sun helped predict and optimize harvest and planting times for crops.

Stage two of your visit is the planetarium, where tour guides explain the Southern Hemisphere's starscapes via both Inca and Greek constellations using the surrounding dome. Inca astronomers saw two sets of constellations: traditional dot-to-dot star shapes and dark cloud constellations within the Milky Way, which largely represented animals, such as a llama or toad.

This intel comes in handy as you transition to Planetarium Cusco's final stage, stargazing. The museum has multiple high-powered telescopes with guided cosmic viewing to bring these ancient astronomy beliefs to life.

OPPOSITE: **The city of Cusco comes to life in a wash of light as night descends.**

TRINIDAD AND TOBAGO

CANBOULAY REENACTMENTS

Celebrate Carnival's past, present, and future.

BUDGET: $ **WHEN TO GO:** February   **ACTIVITY LEVEL:** Mild   **GO FOR:** Culture

Colorful Carnival is synonymous with cheery floats, bedazzled costumes, music, dancing, and around-the-clock parties. But this festival is about more than fun and games. There's a resilient Afro-Caribbean history behind the world-renowned street parade, particularly in its place of origin, Trinidad and Tobago. To learn about it, set a predawn alarm for the Canboulay reenactment, which is held around 4 a.m. in Port of Spain's downtown the Friday before Carnival's kickoff.

The pre-Carnival Canboulay reenactment brings the event's past to life. Dozens of descendants of freed enslaved peoples join together to reenact the historic Canboulay riots in a show of flames, stick fighting, drumming, narration, and a parade. And you can be one of the hundreds of wide-eyed spectators absorbing the festival's history from the bleachers above.

Carnival dates back to the late 18th century when French colonists and enslaved Africans came in droves to the island of Trinidad. Every year between Christmas and Lent, the French celebrated raucously with masquerade balls, known as fêtes. It was a time to get the merriment out of their systems before Lent's 40 days of somber and religious reflection commenced. While the French partied their hearts out, the enslaved weren't allowed to partake—but that didn't stop them. Instead, they launched fêtes of their own.

WHILE YOU'RE THERE

Colonizers banned African percussion music after the Canboulay riots in 1881, but the emancipated improvised with frying pans and trash can lids to create steelpan music, which has evolved over the past century. Enjoy this genre via Panorama, which kicks off the Saturday before Carnival.

OPPOSITE: Carnival revelers dance through the streets in intricate costumes.

PAGES 386-387: Actors from a theater collective perform the annual reenactment of the historical Canboulay.

They called their merriment Canboulay, stemming from the French term *cannes brulées*, for "burnt canes," as the festivities occurred during the sugarcane harvest season. They hosted Canboulay parties to celebrate their culture and mock their oppressors—poking fun at their fancy dress and harsh punishments. But they also used this celebration to share and pass down stories from their homeland. The Canboulay events centered on oral history, traditional stick-fighting dances, and calypso music, a folk-style art form that integrates lively beats and soulful lyrics.

The French masquerades and secret Canboulay fêtes went on for decades until the enslaved gained their freedom in the early 1800s. Even after emancipation, the formerly enslaved hit the streets the night before French Carnival to celebrate their freedom while reminding the largely white festival revelers of the trauma they'd caused. British colonizers saw this revelry as a threat and banned certain elements of the events, such as percussion and singing in public. The Afro-Caribbean revelers adapted different musical genres, such as steelpan music with industrial drums, in an act of defiance.

Things came to a head in 1881, when British police swarmed the Canboulay events in Trinidad. The freed people fought back in what became a bloody battle, now known as the Canboulay riots.

Today's Friday predawn Canboulay reenactments ensure this history is not forgotten. It's a relatively new addition to Trinidad's Carnival; the reenactments began in the early 2000s.

PANTANAL NIGHT SAFARI

Admire an action-packed wetland at its wildest.

BUDGET: $$–$$$$$ **WHEN TO GO:** May–September   **ACTIVITY LEVEL:** Intermediate   **GO FOR:** Wildlife

Climb aboard a 4×4 for one of South America's most fascinating after-dark outings. A twilight journey through the Pantanal, the largest tropical wetland in the world, ups your chances of spotting oft hidden creatures such as jaguars, Brazilian tapirs, nine-banded armadillos, and giant anteaters. And with a swampy grassland backdrop like virtually nowhere else on Earth, this is an experience you won't soon forget.

This more than 70,000-square-mile (181,000 km²) seasonal floodplain, roughly the size of Washington State, extends into Brazil, Bolivia, and Paraguay. Thousands of plant types and abundant animal species, including the world's largest concentration of crocodiles, call these verdant wilds home. The majority of fauna stir from dusk to dawn, says André Moratelli, wildlife biologist and co-owner of Brazil-based Pantanal Jaguar Safaris, which runs night jaunts throughout the wetlands.

Brazil contains 78 percent of the enthralling Pantanal and is the best jumping-off point for a safari. Its stretch of the wetlands spans two Brazilian states, Mato Grosso and Mato Grosso du Sol. Each offers a unique Pantanal experience with the chance for after-hours outings, but Moratelli notes Mato Grosso has the best odds for spotting big cats like jaguars. They're often visible during the dry season, from May to September.

OPPOSITE: Normally an elusive sight, a young jaguar stands in shallow waters of the Pantanal wetlands.

PERU

CLIFF CAMPING

Sleep on a sheer rock face in Peru's Sacred Valley.

BUDGET: $$$ **WHEN TO GO:** Year-round **ACTIVITY LEVEL:** Strenuous **GO FOR:** Adventure

You can enjoy Peru's cosmos from ground-level accommodations— or you could snag a star-saturated night in one of the world's first hanging hotels. To enjoy the latter, head to Skylodge Adventure Suites in Peru's Sacred Valley, where a smattering of glass-walled pods dot a sheer cliff 1,000 feet (305 m) aboveground.

This spine-tingling glamping experience takes a luxury twist on cliff camping—an overnight hack rock climbers use to catch some shut-eye while pursuing major routes, such as the multiday ascent of Yosemite National Park's El Capitan.

It's a hair-raising journey to even reach Skylodge in the first place. You'll climb up a cliffside via ferrata (a series of ladders, ropes, and hooks built into the cliff), or take a zip-line hike to reach the lodge base camp. After arrival, it's time to unwind in your abode: a hanging capsule made of aerospace aluminum and weather-resistant polycarbonate, with soaring views across Inca ruins, such as the Ollantaytambo terraces.

Skylodge has one main dining capsule and three pods, each roughly 24 feet (7 m) in length—enough room for four single beds, or one queen and two singles, plus an eco-toilet and sink. The newest addition, Starlodge offers more easily reachable and pampered cliff digs, with pod access via stairs and a spa connected to the rooms by a bridge.

OPPOSITE: The valley views are worth the trek to reach your Skylodge dome dangling from a cliff face in Peru's Sacred Valley.

ASTRONOMICAL SIGHTSEEING

The night sky's attractions are ever rotating, from planet sightings to meteor showers, or the ultimate astrotourism highlight: a solar eclipse. Some of the many interstellar events and sightings to monitor include:

SOLAR ECLIPSE

This bucket-list astronomical event hits when the moon overlaps the sun. The moon's close-to-Earth orbit makes the space rock large enough to fully cover virtually the entirety of the sun, save its fiery fringes. To see a total solar eclipse, you'll have to watch from the path of totality—a narrow ribbon where the phenomenon of the full moon covering the sun is visible. Those within the path of totality will experience daytime temporarily turning into dusk. Roughly two to five solar eclipses occur each year, although not all are easily visible.

LUNAR ECLIPSE

A lunar eclipse is the more common of the two main eclipse types. It occurs when Earth sits directly between the full moon and the sun. The moon crosses through the shadow of Earth, which gradually covers the moon, turning it from a full orb down to a sliver, then sheer darkness. Unlike solar eclipses, you don't need to be in a slim totality path to see a lunar eclipse. The marvel lasts for hours and is visible anywhere within Earth's night side.

METEOR SHOWER

Few night sky events delight like a meteor shower, when dozens, or even hundreds, of soaring meteors fly across the sky every hour. These "shooting stars" are actually rocky debris from a comet slamming into Earth's atmosphere. The meteors stem from a radiant point in the sky and are named for the constellation where they originate. The brightest meteors, known as fireballs, create a colorful streak across the sky.

SUPERMOON

During a supermoon, the moon appears brighter and larger than normal. Several conditions are required for a supermoon to occur. First, you need a full moon. Next, you need a night when the moon is at its closest approach to Earth, called perigee. The moon reaches its perigee (and its apogee, its furthest point from Earth) once during every 27-day cycle. Supermoon conditions typically align a few times each year; on these nights, the moon can appear 30 percent brighter and 14 percent larger than a typical full moon.

PLANET SIGHTINGS

Throughout the year, you may spot one or multiple planets in the dusk, night, or predawn sky. Some, such as Mars and Venus, are even visible in light-polluted cities. Because the planets travel around the sun at different speeds, we can see our interstellar neighbors at different times of the year. An easy way to distinguish between stars and planets? The former twinkle, the latter don't. Depending on the inkiness of the sky, at certain times you can see Mercury, Mars, Jupiter, Saturn, and Venus without a telescope—Venus, in particular, as it is the brightest planet in our solar system.

COMETS

Prepare to be awestruck if a comet sighting is in the forecast. Although you can see about a dozen comets a year with an amateur telescope, major sightings visible to the naked eye only occur roughly every five to 10 years. These large collections of dust and ice, known for their long tails, are remnants of our solar system's formation.

CONSTELLATIONS AND ASTERISMS

Constellations are a set of stars that, when linked together, create the outline of what looks like certain objects, figures, or animals. There are 88 officially recognized constellations; many of which were named millennia ago, such as the Southern Cross, or Crux, an icon of the Southern Hemisphere night sky that's visible year-round. Early cultures relied on constellations to track time and aid in navigation, and they also incorporated them into their spirituality. An asterism is a newer and more informal set of star patterns that are widely known, such as the Big Dipper, located in the Ursa Major constellation, which is visible year-round and brightest in the spring.

AURORAS

The northern and southern lights, known as aurora borealis and aurora australis, respectively, occur near the north and south geomagnetic poles. Each is caused by a storm of plasma and magnetic energy on the sun, known as a coronal mass ejection (CME). A CME flings charged particles into space via solar winds; when those elements hit Earth's atmosphere, they attract toward the poles, then interact with gases in our atmosphere, such as oxygen and nitrogen. The particle-atmosphere reaction generates a kaleidoscope of colors that streak the sky, which astrotourists trot to Earth's farthest corners to see.

MILKY WAY

Our home galaxy, the Milky Way, is an enchanting highlight of the night sky. Earth occupies just a sliver of this massive spiral galaxy of stars, dust, and gas that appears as a band of concentrated light in the sky. (Scientists believe the Milky Way alone has thousands of planetary systems beyond our own. The observable universe could contain trillions of galaxies—and many more beyond that.) In the United States, the bright, vivid core of the Milky Way is visible from spring through fall. You need a dark sky with minimal light pollution for optimal viewing. In fact, artificial light now prevents roughly one-third of the planet's population from seeing the Milky Way.

DESTINATIONS BY LOCATION

ACKNOWLEDGMENTS

It's been a winding path from a nine-to-five office job to experiencing and writing about some of the world's greatest adventures for a living. I'm forever grateful to the family, friends, and fellow creatives who helped me navigate it.

To my husband, Frank, who's supported me every step (even when it means joining me on late nights in less than ideal conditions—oh, the stories we'll have to share!). To my mom, the most talented writer I know. Thanks for inspiring my pursuits in journalism and travel, and teaching me the art of getting lost. To my brother, who promised to help support me if my career leap of faith didn't work. Your assurance gave me the confidence to give this all a go. To my dog and office assistant, Harry, your pro bono pet therapy throughout this writing process has been very much appreciated. And, of course, to my dad. You inspired everyone around you to be kinder, think bigger, and love the world. I miss you every day.

Writing for National Geographic—a brand so aligned with my passions: exploration, curiosity, and conservation—is a dream. A big thanks to my first *National Geographic Travel* editor, Starlight Williams, for taking a chance on me years ago, and continuing to today. To the editor of this book, Allyson Johnson: I cannot thank you enough for your kindness, enthusiasm, and savvy editing throughout this process. You truly have a gift! And, to the entire National Geographic team behind the book— designer Anne LeongSon, photo editor Uliana Bazar, production editor Michael O'Connor, creative director Elisa Gibson—thank you for bringing these words to life.

This book would be nothing without the myriad local experts who shared their worlds with me. People are the best part of any travel experience, and each and every one of you proves why. Thank you, thank you for inviting us in.

ABOUT THE AUTHOR

Stephanie Vermillion is a freelance journalist and photographer. She covers astrotourism, adventure travel, and conservation. Her work has appeared in *National Geographic, Outside, Travel + Leisure,* BBC Travel, *Afar,* and the World Wildlife Fund's *World Wildlife* magazine, among many other publications. She's reported on stories in some of the world's wildest and most remote places, from camping on the Greenland ice sheet during a snowstorm to following a group of Indigenous sea turtle conservationists on the shores of northern Panama.

When she's not writing, traveling, or fighting sleep for "just a few more minutes" of watching the northern lights or stars, Stephanie spends her time hiking, cycling, and paddling in the great outdoors with her husband and fellow adventure buffs (although she's equally happy reading and sipping coffee on the couch with her dog, Harry).

Find Stephanie on Instagram (@bystephanievermillion) or her website, *stephanievermillionstudio.com.*

ILLUSTRATIONS CREDITS

Cover, Pete Lomchid/Getty Images; back cover, Tim Draper/Sime/eStock Photo; 2-3, Michael Uthe/500px/Getty Images; 4-5, Joe McNally/National Geographic Image Collection; 7, Pete McBride/National Geographic Image Collection; 8-9, Andrea De Silva/Reuters/Redux; 10-1, Frans Lanting/National Geographic Image Collection; 13, Daniel Viñe Garcia/Cavan Images; 14-5, Nisangha/Getty Images; 17, R. Tyler Gross/Aurora Open RF/Alamy Stock Photo; 18-9, Marc Guitard/Getty Images; 21, Pyngodan@gmail.com/Getty Images; 22-3, Michael Baynes/Getty Images; 25, photo by Seyiram Kweku (@seyiram) on Unsplash; 27, J. Ritterbach/juniors@wildlife/Alamy Stock Photo; 28-9, Frans Lanting/National Geographic Image Collection; 30, Frank Herholdt/Getty Images; 31, Shaun Stanley/Alamy Stock Photo; 33, Kim Marriott/Alamy Stock Photo; 34-5, EcoPic/Getty Images; 37, Jason_YU/Getty Images; 38-9, George Steinmetz/National Geographic Image Collection; 41, Bill Curtsinger/National Geographic Image Collection; 43, Vlad Sokhin; 45, Nick Brundle Photography/Getty Images; 46-7, Kenneth Garrett/National Geographic Image Collection; 49, Michael S. Lewis/Getty Images; 50-1, bjdlzx/Getty Images; 53, bingdian/Getty Images; 54-5, zorazhuang/Getty Images; 56, Bernd Grundmann/Huber/eStock Photo; 57, bjdlzx/Getty Images; 59, John Holmes/Alamy Stock Photo; 60-1, MEMEME/Alamy Stock Photo; 63, kecl/Getty Images; 64-5, Horizon Images/Alamy Stock Photo; 67, Ye Aung Thu/AFP via Getty Images; 68-9, U Aung/Xinhua via Getty Images; 71, Gavin Hellier/robertharding; 73, kayakasiaPh x Aplaya; 75, Brian Skerry/National Geographic Image Collection; 76-7, ma-mi/Getty Images; 79, Teera Konakan/Getty Images; 80-1, porkio photograph/Getty Images; 82, Adrian P Young/Stocksy; 83, onuma Inthapong/Getty Images; 85, Stocktrek Images/Getty Images; 87, Alexander Grabchilev/Stocksy; 88-9, Jak Wonderly/National Geographic Image Collection; 90, Brendan Hoffman/National Geographic Image Collection; 91, Alison Wright/National Geographic Image Collection; 93, Mint Images/Art Wolfe/Getty Images; 94-5, Dream Lover/Stocksy; 97, Anupam Mukherjee/500px/Getty Images; 99, Keith Ladzinski; 100-1, Jake Norton/Cavan Images; 102, Mark Fisher/National Geographic Image Collection; 103, Max Lowe/National Geographic Image Collection; 105, Markus Kirchgessner/laif/Redux; 107, Nora de Angelli; 108-9, Darby Sawchuk; 111, Antonello Lanzellotto/AGF/Alamy Stock Photo; 112-3, Norbert Eisele-Hein/imageBROKER/Alamy Stock Photo; 115, Reinhard Dirscherl/Cavan Images; 116-7, AtanasBozhikovNasko/Getty Images; 118, Manfred Bortoli/Sime/eStock Photo; 119, Filippo Bacci/Getty Images; 120-1, Stephen Alvarez/National Geographic Image Collection; 123, an Woitas/picture alliance via Getty Images; 124-5, Daniel Karmann/picture alliance via Getty Images; 126, Gunter Hartmann/Sime/eStock Photo; 127, fotografixx/Getty Images; 129, Lukas Jonaitis/Shutterstock; 131, Brandon Huttenlocher/Cavan Images; 132-3, Sarote Pruksachat/Getty Images; 134, Russell Edwards/Getty Images; 135, Armand Ahmed Tamboly/Sime/eStock Photo; 137, Stefano Politi Markovina/Sime/eStock Photo; 138-9, Gonzalo Azumendi/Getty Images; 141, Xseon/Shutterstock; 143, Nicolas Vera-Ortiz/Getty Images; 144-5, ASMR/Getty Images; 147, Antony Del Vecchio/Alamy Stock Photo; 149, Franco Cogoli/Sime/eStock Photo; 150-1, wanderluster/Getty Images; 153, Robert Clark; 154-5, Andy Buchanan/Alamy Stock Photo; 156, Jerome Lorieau/Sime/eStock Photo; 157, AndrewJ/Adobe Stock; 159, Andreas Mohaupt/Getty Images; 160-1, Robbie Shone/Alamy Stock Photo; 163, Gennaro Caninchello/Alamy Stock Photo; 165, Babak Tafreshi/National Geographic Image Collection; 166-7, Miguel Claro/Science Photo Library; 169, Victoria Jones/PA Images/Alamy Stock Photo; 171, Westend61/A. Tamboly/Alamy Stock Photo; 173, George Pachantouris/Getty Images; 175, Luigi Vaccarella/Sime/eStock Photo; 177, Nick Venton/500px/Getty Images; 179, Matt Williams-Ellis/Sime/eStock Photo; 181, frantic00/Shutterstock; 182-3, Jan Wlodarczyk/Sime/eStock Photo; 185, elxeneize/Getty Images;

187, Reda and Co/Alamy Stock Photo; 188–190, Keith Ladzinski/National Geographic Image Collection; 191, Morten Flarup Andersen/Cavan Images; 193, De Meester Johan/Arterra Picture Library/Alamy Stock Photo; 194–5, Johnathan Ampersand Esper/Cavan Images; 196–7, Nick Fox/Alamy Stock Photo; 199, imageBROKER/E. Baccega/Alamy Stock Photo; 200–1, Yvette Cardozo/Alamy Stock Photo; 203, WorldFoto/Alamy Stock Photo;204–5, Paul Nicklen/National Geographic Image Collection; 207, Alan Dyer/Stocktrek Images/Alamy Stock Photo; 209, Alex Trautwig/MLB via Getty Images; 211, Jim Vallee/Getty Images; 213, Daniel Osterkamp/Getty Images; 214–5, Robert Garrigus/Alamy Stock Photo; 216, Babak Tafreshi/National Geographic Image Collection; 217, Ben Horton/National Geographic Image Collection; 219, LanaG/Alamy Stock Photo; 221, Jacob Boomsma/Getty Images; 222–3, Mike Shaw; 224, Jim Brandenburg/Minden Pictures; 225, Rob Schultz/Adobe Stock; 227, Adrian Davies/Alamy Stock Photo; 228–9, Keith Ladzinski/National Geographic Image Collection; 231, Mario Tama/Getty Images; 233, Noam Galai/Getty Images; 234–5, Alexi Rosenfeld/Getty Images; 237, Russell Kord Archive/Alamy Stock Photo; 238–9, Amanda Mustard/The New York Times/Redux; 241, Walter Bibikow/eStock Photo; 242–3, Ted Spiegel/National Geographic Image Collection; 245, Gabriel Jaime Jimenez/eStock Photo; 246–7, Greg Balfour Evans/Alamy Stock Photo; 249, Adam Mowery/Tandem Stock; 250–1, Michael R Turner/Alamy Stock Photo; 253, Panther Media/Alamy Stock Photo; 255, Floris van Breugel/naturepl/Alamy Stock Photo; 256–7, Babak Tafreshi/National Geographic Image Collection; 258, Joshua Moore/Getty Images; 259, Shawn Poynter/The New York Times/Redux; 261, LWA/Getty Images; 262–3, Robbie Shone/National Geographic Image Collection; 264, Michael Nichols/National Geographic Image Collection; 265, Phil Schermeister/National Geographic Image Collection; 267, Stephen Frink/Getty Images; 268–9, Michael Patrick O'Neill/Alamy Stock Photo; 270, Blue Planet Archive SKO/Alamy Stock Photo; 271, Dave Williams/Getty Images; 273, Jim Havey/Alamy Stock Photo; 275, Pete McBride/National Geographic Image Collection; 276–7, Bill Hatcher/National Geographic Image Collection; 279, Elizabeth M. Ruggiero/Getty Images; 281, Doug Perrine/Alamy Stock Photo; 282–3, Scott Sady; 285, Patrick Kelley/National Geographic Image Collection; 286–7, Quek Zong Ye; 289, David Liittschwager/National Geographic Image Collection; 290–1, WireStock/Alamy Stock Photo; 293–5, Michiel van Noppen; 297, Mark Pollard/Stocksy; 298–9, Loes Kieboom/Shutterstock; 301, Simon Norfolk/National Geographic Image Collection; 303–5, Visit Panamá; 307, Lynn Willis of High South Creative; 308–9, Charles O. Cecil/Alamy Stock Photo; 310–1, John White Photos/Getty Images; 313, Mathias Rhode/Alamy Stock Photo; 314–5, Aldo Pavan/Sime/eStock Photo; 317, james_stone76/Shutterstock; 318–9, Pavel Dudek/Alamy Stock Photo; 321, Andreas Ruhz/Alamy Stock Photo; 322–3, courtesy of Phillip Island Nature Parks; 325, David Doubilet/National Geographic Image Collection; 326–7, Norbert Probst/imageBROKER/Alamy Stock Photo; 328, Travelscape Images/Alamy Stock Photo; 329, Marica van der Meer/Alamy Stock Photo; 331, Lea Scaddan/Getty Images; 332–3, Juergen Freund/Nature Picture Library; 335, Visions from Earth/Alamy Stock Photo; 337, Matteo Colombo/Getty Images; 339, Andrew Coleman/Alamy Stock Photo; 340–1, Glen Butler; 342, DestinationsInNewZealand/Shutterstock; 343, Danny Rood, IG @de_rood; 345, Geoff Renner/robertharding; 346–7, Paul Nicklen/National Geographic Image Collection; 348, Yuri Choufour/DanitaDelimont/Alamy Stock Photo; 349, Michael Nolan/robertharding; 351, Jaynes Gallery/DanitaDelimont/Alamy Stock Photo; 352–3, Charly Lataste/Hemis/Alamy Stock Photo; 354, Walter Meayers Edwards/National Geographic Image Collection; 355, Paul Nicklen/National Geographic Image Collection; 357, Michael Melford/National Geographic Image Collection; 358–9, Michael Runkel/robertharding; 360–1, abriendomundo/Getty Images; 363, Imago/Alamy Stock Photo; 365, Pakawat Thongcharoen/Getty Images; 366–7, Michael Breitung/Huber/eStock Photo; 369, Hispanolistic/Getty Images; 370–1, Genaro Palacios/VWPics/Redux; 373–6, Babak Tafreshi/National Geographic Image Collection; 377, Eric Hanson/Getty Images; 379, Heeb Photos/eStock Photo; 380–1, Steve Winter/National Geographic Image Collection; 383, Carl Forbes/Alamy Stock Photo; 385, S. Falke/laif/Redux; 386–7, Sean Drakes/Alamy Stock Photo; 389, Uwe-Bergwitz/Getty Images; 391, Pilar Olivares/Reuters/Redux.

Since 1888, the National Geographic Society has funded more than 14,000 research, conservation, education, and storytelling projects around the world. National Geographic Partners distributes a portion of the funds it receives from your purchase to National Geographic Society to support programs including the conservation of animals and their habitats.

Get closer to National Geographic Explorers and photographers, and connect with our global community. Join us today at nationalgeographic.org/joinus

Library of Congress Cataloging-in-Publication Data
Names: Vermillion, Stephanie, author.
Title: 100 nights of a lifetime : the world's ultimate adventures after dark / Stephanie Vermillion.
Other titles: One hundred nights of a lifetime
Description: Washington, D.C. : National Geographic, 2024. I Includes index. I Summary: "In this one-of-a-kind illustrated collection, discover 100 after-dark adventures around the world"-- Provided by publisher.
Identifiers: LCCN 2023056813 I ISBN 9781426223372 (hardback)
Subjects: LCSH: Nightlife--Cross-cultural studies. I Night--Social aspects--Cross-cultural studies. I City and town life--Cross-cultural studies.
Classification: LCC GT3408 .V47 2024 I DDC 307.76--dc23/eng/20240223
LC record available at https://lccn.loc.gov/2023056813

The information in this book has been carefully checked and to the best of our knowledge is accurate. However, details are subject to change, and the publisher cannot be responsible for such changes, or for errors or omissions. Assessments of sites, hotels, and restaurants are based on the author's subjective opinions, which do not necessarily reflect the publisher's opinion.

Printed in South Korea

24/QPSK/1